The Lotus Symbol In Indian Literature and Art

Santona Basu

Originals
(an imprint of Low Price Publications)
Delhi-110052

Distributed By
D.K. Publishers Distributors (P) Ltd.
4834/24, Ansari Road, Darya Ganj,
New Delhi-110002
Phones: 3278584, 3278368, 3261465,
e-mail: dkpd@del3.vsnl.net.in
visit us at: www.dkpd.com

First Published 2002
ISBN 81-7536-288-X

Published By
Originals
(an imprint of Low Price Publications)
A-6, Nimri Commercial Centre,
Near Ashok Vihar Phase-IV,
Delhi-110052
Phones: 7401672, 7452453
e-mail: lpp@nde.vsnl.net.in
visit us at: www.lppindia.com

Printed At:
D K Fine Art Press P Ltd.
Delhi-110052

PRINTED IN INDIA

For My Family

PREFACE

In the year 1961 a fellowship from the German Academic Exchange Service (DAAD) enabled me to go to Germany for higher studies in Indology under the guidance of the late Prof. Dr. E. Waldschmidt, the then Director of the Indologisches Seminar of Goettingen University. He suggested the topic regarding lotus flower in the ancient Indian literature, which was readily accepted by me, the reason being I was always intrigued by the abundance of this flower in visual art, particularly of ancient India. There most of the Hindu divinities and the Buddha have been allotted a lotus seat. *Why*? My quest for finding the root cause for the preferential treatment apportioned to lotus, started from the earliest of Indian literature viz. the Vedas and its subsequent books known as *Brāhmaṇas, Āraṇyakas* and *Upaniṣads* and stretched to the books of Pāli Canons for interpreting lotus in the Buddhist art. The result of the conclusion was my thesis, *The Lotus in the Vedic and Canonical Pali Literature.* This monograph is a revised and rearranged version of my thesis.

The present work, embracing the Vedic and Pāli Canonical texts and sculptures, attempts to make understandable both to the students and general readers, how the ancient Indian mind visualised this water-born flower, reflections of which are contained in the ancient texts and plastic art.

An attempt has also been made to classify the common Sanskrit names of the lotus based on meagre scientific data that could be gleaned from the literary works of the classical Sanskrit period.

My thanks go to Dr. K.R. Pal of Meerut University for his valuable suggestions while writing my thesis and to my son Anirvan and daughter-in-law Anuradha for giving this monograph its final shape. Lastly, I am thankful to the Directors of the National Museum and Archaeological Survey of India, New Delhi for the supply of the photographs.

BANGALORE SANTONA BASU

SEPTEMBER, 2002

Contents

List of Illustrations

List of Plates

Abbreviations

AN	Aṅguttaranikāya
AV	Atharva-Veda
Ch.U.	Chāndogya Upaniṣad
DN	Dīghanikāya
Mn	Mahāniddesa
MN	Majjhimanikāya
MS	Maitrāyaṇī Saṁhitā
MU	Maitrāyaṇī Upaniṣad
PB	Pañcaviṁśa Brāhmaṇa
RV	Ṛg-Veda
SN	Saṁyuttanikāya
SB	Śatapatha Brāhmaṇa
TA	Taittirīya Āraṇyaka
TB	Taittirīya Brāhmaṇa
TS	Taittirīya Saṁhitā
VS	Vājasneyī Saṁhitā

1

INTRODUCTION

The Vedic literature is a veritable storehouse of seeds of Indian thoughts, which in the later periods assumed the shapes of huge trees with innumerable branches. This is true also in the case of the association of lotus with deities. Gods and goddesses carved in stones are artistic interpretations of the descriptions of deities given in the various Purāṇas, which are considered as records of history and mythology of ancient India.[1] The seeds of these ideas were existent in the Vedic times, which are evident from the literature of that age. Hence the images of Hindu pantheon have been explained in the light of Vedic literature. The Vedic literature comprises of the four Vedas - *Ṛg-Veda, Sāma-Veda, Atharva-Veda* and *Yajur-Veda* (with its two schools - Black and White), the *Brāhmaṇas, Āraṇyakas* and *Upaniṣads*. This period spans around five centuries from the sixth or fifth century to the first century BC. Apparently the Vedic people were not idolaters as till date archaeologists have not unearthed images belonging to that period, though the Vedic gods and goddesses were attributed with anthropomorphic qualities in the hymns of the Vedas.

After the Vedic period Buddhism dominated the Indian scene in religion, culture and literature. Texts of that period known as Pāli Canons represent that phase of Indian history, which starts from the end of the first century BC and 'covers some five centuries of literary development'.[2] The help of Pāli

---

1 Cf. *Cultural Heritage of India*, Vol. II, p. 240 ff.
2 Cf. *Cultural Heritage of India*, Vol. 1, p. 443.

Canonical texts have been taken for interpreting the role of lotus in Buddhist works of art. In the sculptures of that period one comes across this flower at every turn of head either as the seat of the Buddha or as a decorative motif. The relation between Buddhism and lotus as presented in the plastic art has been explained with the help of references to lotus in the Pāli Canons, which are generally known by the name *Tipiṭaka* (Sans. *Tripiṭaka*). *Tipiṭaka* or the 'Three Baskets' consists of "collections of speeches or conversations, of sayings, songs, narratives and rules of the Order.[3]

The names of the three *piṭakas* are:

Vinayapiṭaka – Basket of discipline of the Order

Suttapiṭaka – Basket of *sūtras* or sermons

Abhidhammapiṭaka – Basket of higher subtleties of the doctrine[4]

Vinayapiṭaka again comprises of:

1. *Suttavibhaṅga* – (i) *Mahāvibhaṅga* and (ii) *Bhikkhunīvibhaṅga*

2. The *Khandakās* – (i) *Mahāvagga* and (ii) *Cullavagga*

3. The *Parivāra* or *Parivārapāṭha*.

The *Suttapiṭaka* consists of five *nikāyas* or collections. These are:

(i) Dīghanikāya, (ii) *Majjhimanikāya*, (iii) *Saṁyuttanikāya*, (iv) *Aṅguttaranikāya* and (v) *Khuddakanikāya*.

Under *Khuddakanikāya* there are fifteen books. Of these *Jātaka, Therīgāthā, Theragāthā, Vimānavatthu, Petavatthu* are of some importance for our discussion.

Abhidhammapiṭaka consists of five collections: (i) *Dhammasaṁgaṇi*, (ii) *Vibhaṅga,* (iii) *Dhātukathā,* (iv) *Puggalapaññāti* and (v) *Kathāvatthu.*

---

3 M. Winternitz, *A History of Indian Literature*, Vol.II, p. 3.
4 *Ibid*, pp. 8-9.

Before embarking on the symbolism of lotus in art and literature it is worthwhile to know this flower from the botanical point of view and the artists way of chiselling it in stones or painting it on the walls of Ajanta caves.

'Lotus' is the popular name of a group of flowers belonging to the family *Nymphaeaceae*, an aquatic plant. Its two genera in India – *Nelumbo* and *Nymphaea* – are commonly known as lotus and water lily respectively. The distinctive characteristics of a lotus (*Nelumbo*) are the shape of its petals, torus and carpels. Carpels are completely free and irregularly sunk in torus as a longitudinal section of the flower shows (Figure 1).

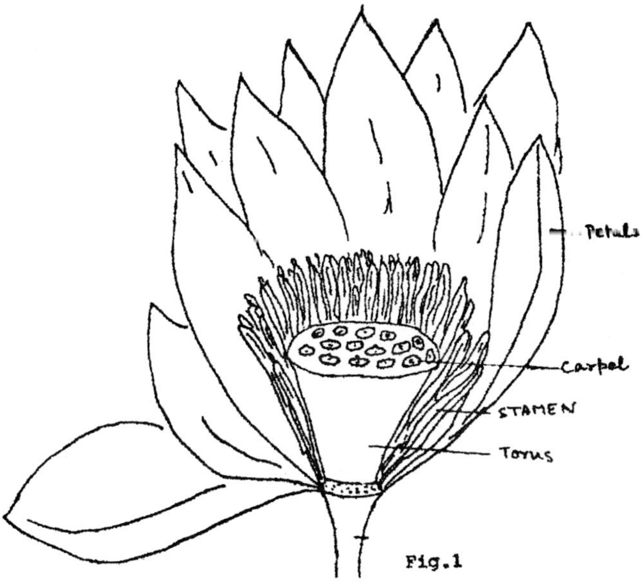

Figure 1

In the visible art lotus has been represented quite faithfully. Although like every other work of art there are some artistic deviations. To some extent this flower has been stylised and abstracted, but its petals, torus and in some cases detached carpels make it possible to identify it with lotus as found in the nature. In the plastic art this flower has been presented from various angles. When shown from above the petals are arranged in two or more rows around the torus and detached carpels are visible (Figures 2 – 5).

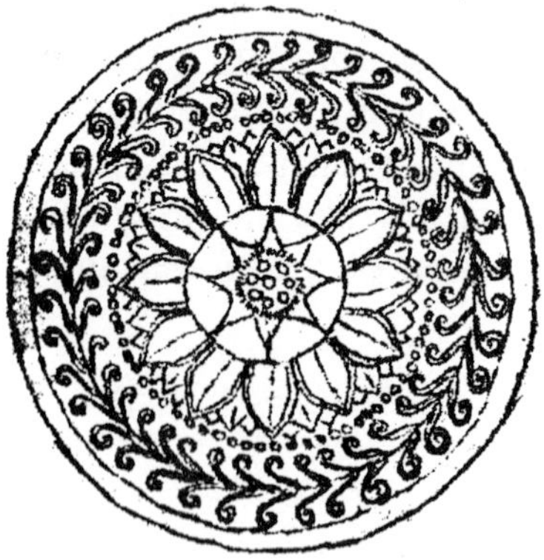

Figure 2: BHARHUT

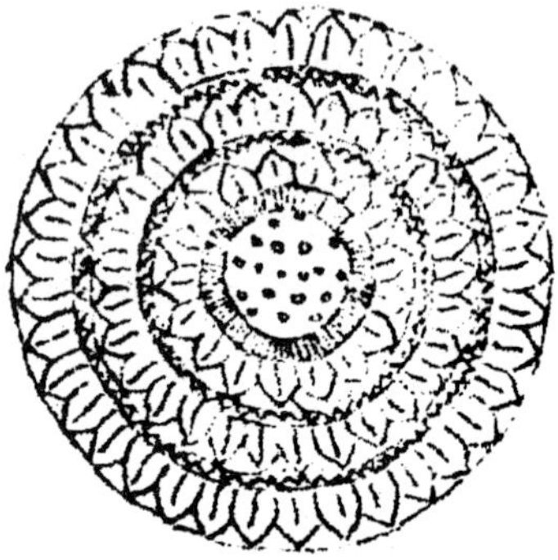

Figure 3: AMARAVATI

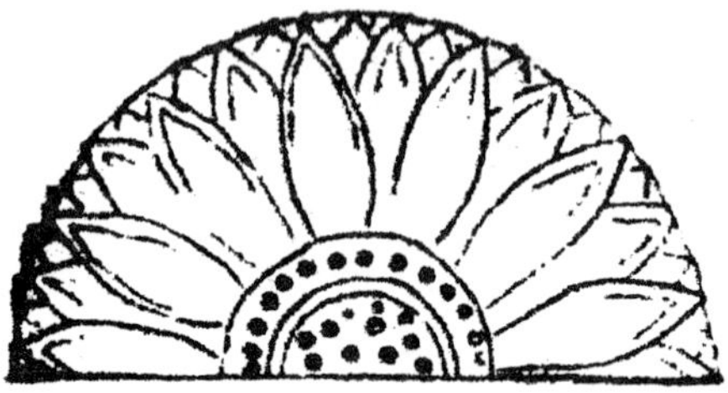

Figure 4: AJANTA

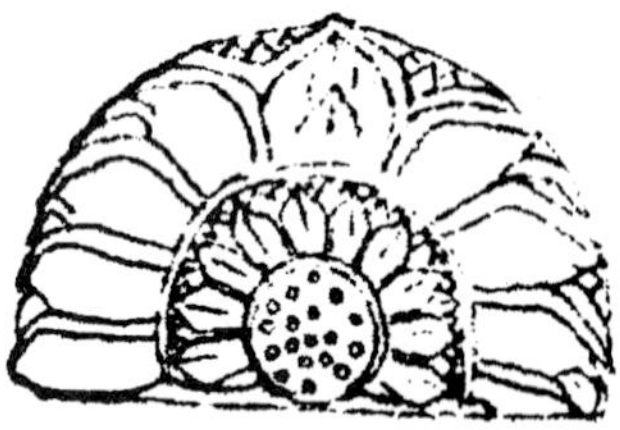

Figure 5: BODHGAYA

The side view of the flower is characterised by a raised torus from the axis of the flower with hanging petals and carpels (Figures 6,7).

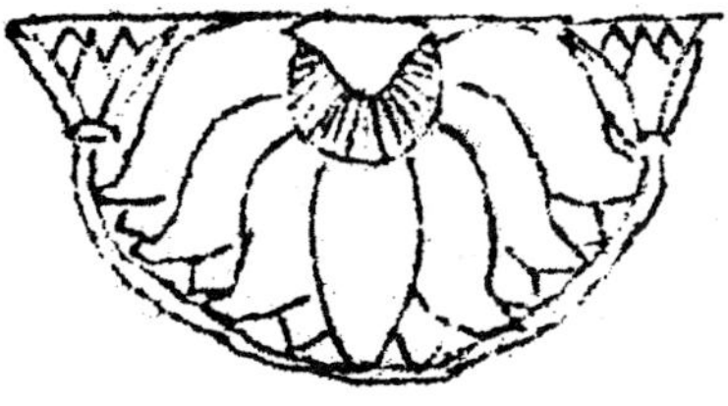

Figure 6: BHARHUT

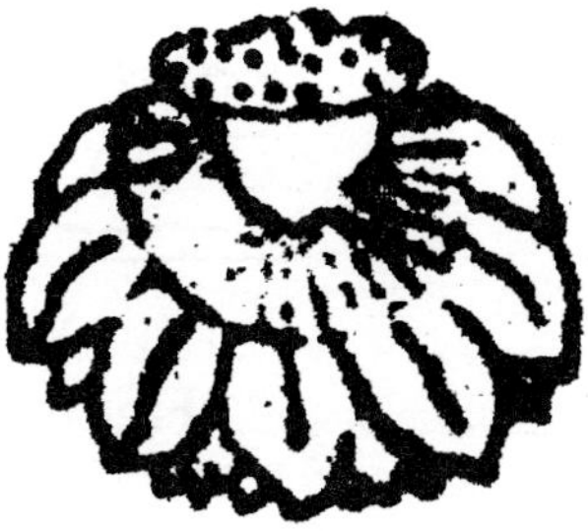

Figure 7: SANCHI STUPA

In some cases where lotus is shown from above, human face or some other motif is carved in the torus instead of carpels. The petals, however, have the same forms as shown in the figures above, which make it obvious, that the lotus flower is meant by such representations.

In art another type of flower comes mostly with the lotus, differentiating itself from the latter by the shape of its petals, which are long and pointed (Figures 8,9,10). This represents water lily (*Nymphaea*), some of the species of which have lanceolate petals[5]. This species is always shown from the side and never isolated. They are carved quite small beside a big open lotus or together with small lotus buds and other decorative motifs (Figures 6, 10, Plate 9).

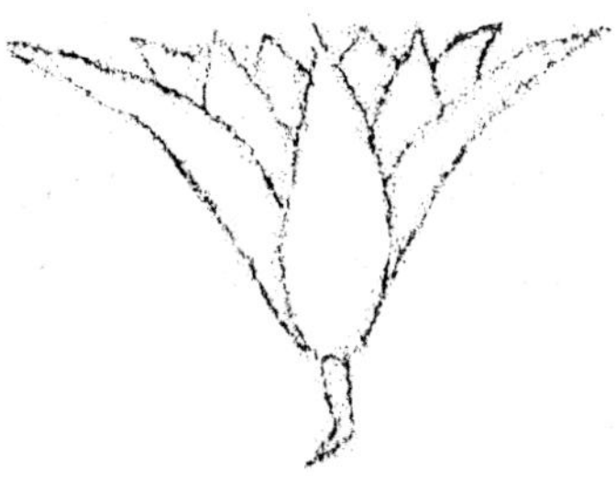

Figure 8: Sanchi, Stupa 1

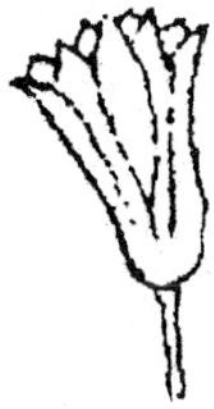

Figure 9: Amaravati

5 See pp. 84.

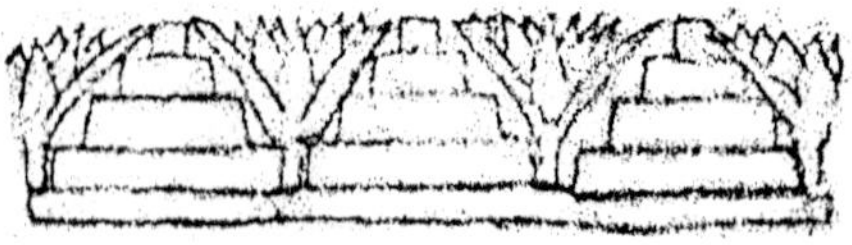

Figure 10: Bharhut

Apart from the stylised representations of this flower sometimes it has been chiselled so faithfully to its model in the nature, that it seems as if the flowers are frozen on stone. Two of its finest examples are a group of lotuses and leaves on the Kushana statuette of Śrī-Lakṣmī and on one of the gates of Sanchi stupa (Plates 11, 13).

Lotus, the favourite flower of the Vedic seers, of the Buddha and his followers, of the iconographers and artists also retains its prime position in the classical Sanskrit literature but primarily as the standard of judgement of human beauty. This role of lotus started from the later Vedic period, sustained through the Buddhist period reached its height in the literary works of the classical period. Human, particularly feminine beauty is set on par with the lotus, the ultimate example of beauty for the poets. The poetic works and plays of this period are replete with such comparisons, where the lotus has been used as an *upamā* (simile). The poets while using the example of the lotus as an *upamā* have sometimes hinted at one or the other botanical data of one of the species of the lotus in some verses to make their statements more forceful. This has led to an attempt to classify the Sanskrit names of the lotus botanically.

The short botanical introduction of lotus and its presentation in art given above will enable us to examine its role in the ancient Indian literature and its reflections in the ancient Indian art, which is unthinkable without lotus, be it as a seat or a decorative motif. To avoid complication the word 'lotus' has been used in the following pages in general for both lotus as well as water lily.

2

Puṣkara

There is a predominance of the lotus flower in association with the various Hindu deities, where it serves as their seats and as decorative motifs in the vast range of ancient Indian art. This leads up to the following question:

Is the lotus flower in Indian art an end in itself, or does it symbolise an assortment of thoughts and conceptions when associated with the deities?

In ancient India art was in no way segregated from literature. The sculptors and iconographers interpreted and transferred the thoughts and conceptions contained in the Vedas and Purāṇas to the plastic art, of course in accordance to the *śilpa śāstras*. It can thus be said, that art was a visual representation of thoughts, which were accumulated in the ancient Indian literature. The portrayal of lotus in Indian art was, therefore, an expression of a vast tradition of gradually developing ideas starting from the most ancient of Indian literature, viz. the Vedas. *Puṣkara* is the earliest denomination of the lotus flower found in the Vedas. This word has been used consistently through out the Vedic literature and particularly in the *Ṛg-Veda*, wherever the poets allude to this flower. Although *puṣkara* is the main word used in the *Ṛg-Veda* to denote lotus, one might ask if it might not have earlier stood for some other object and have later come to represent the lotus. This doubt is laid to rest, as there is a specific reference to the sweet scent of *puṣkara* in a hymn in the *Atharva-Veda*. The hymn is addressed to the Mother Earth, in which the poet wishes various boons from her and one of these is the sweet scent of the Earth, that is found in *puṣkara*: "Thy sweet scent, which entered the *puṣkara*" (*yaste gandhaḥ puṣkaram āviveśa* - AV 12.1.24). Furthermore, in the *Ṛg-Veda* the twin gods Aśvinā are addressed with the epithet 'the lotus-garlanded ones' (*puṣkara-srajau* - RV 10.184.2). The word *puṣkariṇī* (literally means 'abounding in *puṣkara*') denotes a lotus pond and has been used in that sense in the *Ṛg-Veda* as well as in the *Atharva-Veda*. In the *Ṛg*-Veda[6] a poet points to the stirring of a lotus pond touched by wind. The *Atharva-Veda*[7] mentions globular bulbous roots and stalks of a lotus plant in a lotus pond.

2.1 Agni

Agni, the deified fire, mainly the sacrificial fire, of the Vedic mythology is the second most important god of the Vedic pantheon, first being Indra the king of gods. Agni is considered as the intermediary between gods and human beings. He transports offerings and oblations given in the sacrificial fire to the gods for the benefit of the householder and also brings gods to sacrifices. He has various births such as from rubbing dry woods (*araṇi*) for the sacrificial fire. He is also born in the form of the sun as the light of the heaven, in the aerial waters as lightening and from the cosmic waters before the creation. About his birth from the cosmic waters the *Ṛg-Veda* says:

"O, Agni, in the beginning *atharvan* churned thee out of the lotus, the bearer of all"[8]

This is the earliest reference to *puṣkara* in the Vedic literature. *Śatapatha Brāhmaṇa* while explaining this verse says *atharvan* is *prāṇa*: "O Agni, *atharvan* rubbed thee out of the lotus flower'. Lotus flower is indeed water. Breath of life is *atharvan*. Indeed he rubbed it out of the water in the beginning".[9]

---

6 *yathā vātaḥ puṣkariṇīṃ samiṅgayati sarvataḥ* – RV 5.78.7 (as the wind stirs the lotus pond in all directions)

7 *nāsya kṣetre puṣkariṇī nāṇḍikaṁ jāyate bisam* - AV 5.17.16 (not in his field a lotus-pond,the bulb-bearing (lotus) or stalk come into existence.)

8 *tvām agne puṣkarād adhy atharvā niramanthat /*
mūrdhno viśvasya vāghataḥ // RV 6.16.13

9 *tvām agne puṣkarād adhy atharvā niramanthat iti āpo vai puṣkaraṁ prāṇo 'tharvā vā etam agre 'dbhyo niramanthat.* SB 6.4.4.2.

This explanation from Śatapatha Brāhmaṇa says, *atharvā*[10] is same as the 'breath of life', which means, *atharvā* gives breath of life to Agni. In other words, Agni becomes visible with the help of *atharvā*. In the later period of the Vedic literature this theory of the birth of Agni on the lotus (*puṣkara*) was expounded and Prajāpati takes the place of *atharvā*. *Taittirīya Saṁhitā* says:

> In the beginning this was surging (*salilam*) water. Prajāpati becoming wind rocked on the lotus leaf. He could not find any support. He saw the nest of waters. On that he piled Agni. That became this Earth. Then indeed he had support.[11]

According to the Vedic cosmogonical conception, there were only chaotic waters before the creation. "All this was heaving waters", says the *Ṛg-Veda* (*salilaṁ sarvam ā idam* – RV 10.129.3) and *puṣkara* as a water-born flower symbolises that water, the carrier of all in their latent forms. The hymn form the *Ṛg-Veda* (6.16.13) conveys the most important significance of the word *puṣkara*. *Puṣkara* here stands for the chaotic waters that possessed the latent energy for the creation. This hymn says Agni was born on water, i.e. lotus. Hence in the Vedas he has often been called the 'germ or foetus of water'[12] and also "the son of water"[13]

In the passage from the *Taittirīya Saṁhitā*, quoted above, both *puṣkaraparṇam* and *salilam* point to the seemingly contradictory states of the primeval cosmic waters. *Salilam* points to the unsteady and surging waters before the creation and *puṣkara-parṇam* to the power of giving stability latent in the surging waters, which could function as the support of

---

10 *Atharva* or *atharvan* is the name of the priest who is said to have first instituted the worship of fire. Cf *Sans.-Eng. Dictionary* by Monier-Williams. Also see Grassmann, Wörterbuch zum Rigveda.

11 *idam agre salilam āsīt. sa prājapatiḥ puṣkaraparṇe vāto bhūto 'lelāyat. sa pratisṭhāmnāvindat. sa etad apāṁ kulāyam apaśyat. tasmin agnim acinuta. tad iyam abhavat. tato vai sa pratyatiṣṭhat.* TS 5.6.4.2-3

12 *garbhaḥ yaḥ apām* RV 1.70.3; also 3.1.12,13; 7.9.3; AV 13.1.50 etc.

13 *apām napāt* Cf. A.A. Macdonell, *Vedic Mythology*, p. 70

Prajāpati, the Creator. The epithet 'Nest of waters' (*apām kulāyam*) is an allusion to Agni, who was not yet manifested. It alludes to that period of genesis, when it was one with the waters and had no separate existence. 'Prajāpati piled Agni on the nest of waters' means, with the help of Prajāpati Agni was manifested and then became this earth. In the Vedic creation theory Agni and Earth are, so to say, two sides of the same coin. 'This is Agni' affirms *Śatapatha Brāhmaṇa* (*iyam hi agniḥ* – SB 7.4.1.8).

This Vedic conception of the birth of Agni on *puṣkara* is reflected in this 10th century sculpture of Agni standing on a lotus (Plate 1). In connection with Agni lotus signifies the birthplace of this deity with its latent energy for creation as well as the power of executing the role of a support for the creation.

2.2 Cosmogony and Prajāpati

Rooted in this hymn from the *Ṛg-Veda* a creation myth gradually takes shape. "To say in a word", says Winternitz[14], "what renders these hymns so valuable for us, is that we see before us in them a mythology in the making." That holds true regarding the myths about cosmogony. The hymns of the *Ṛg-Veda* are mostly elaborated and explained in the Vedic texts of later period and in that process a myth about creation emerges. On Agni's birth on the lotus *Tattirīya Saṁhitā* comments: "For on the lotus leaf he (Prajāpati) found him (Agni) reposing."[15] The *Śatapatha Brāhmaṇa* goes a step further and weaves a myth around these lines and says that once Agni disappeared from the gods. On being requested by the gods Prajāpati found him on a lotus. Agni was reposing on it, having crept forth from the waters.[16]

---

14 M. Winternitz, *A History of Indian Literature*, Vol. 1, Pt. 1, p. 65

15 *puṣkaraparṇe hy enam upāśritamavindat* – TS 5.1.4.4

16 *agnir devebhya udakrāmat so āpaḥ prāviśat te devāḥ prajāpatim abruvaṁs tvam imam anviccha sa tubhyaṁ svāya pitra āvirbhaviṣyatīti tam aśvaḥ śuklo bhūtvānvaicchat tam adbhya upodāśṛtaṁ puṣkaraparṇe viveda.* SB 7.3.2.14

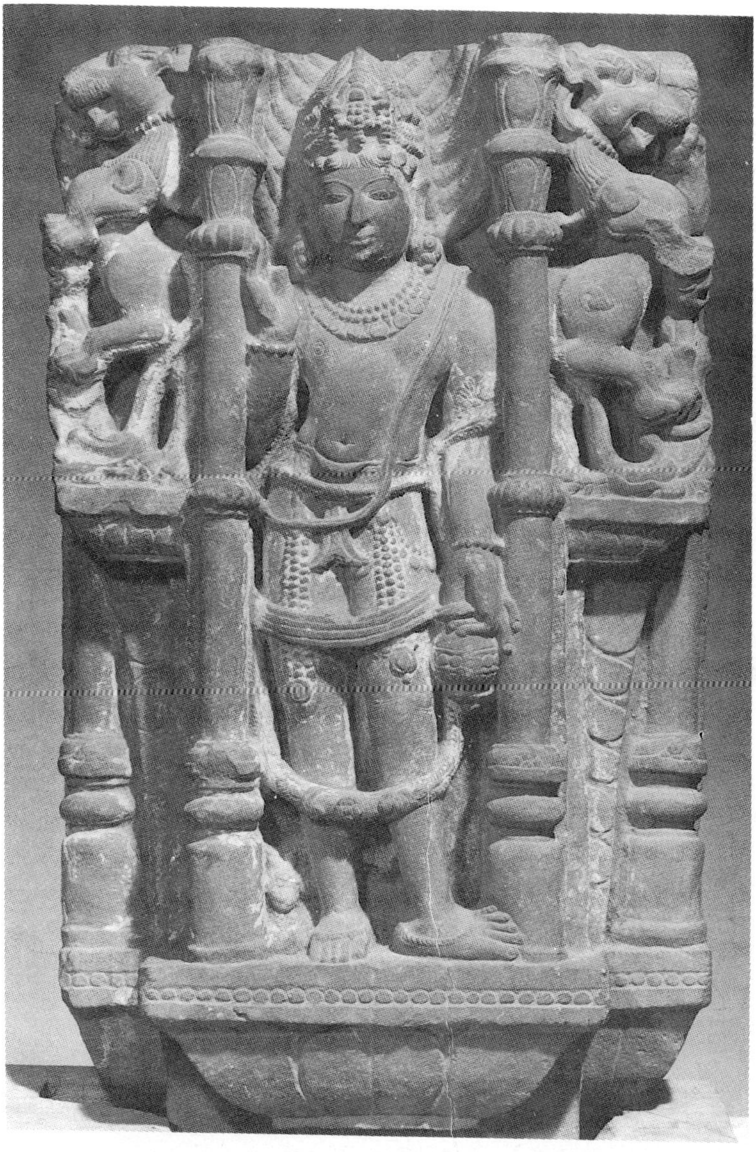

Plate 1: Agni on Lotus, Pratihara (U.P.), 10th C. AD.

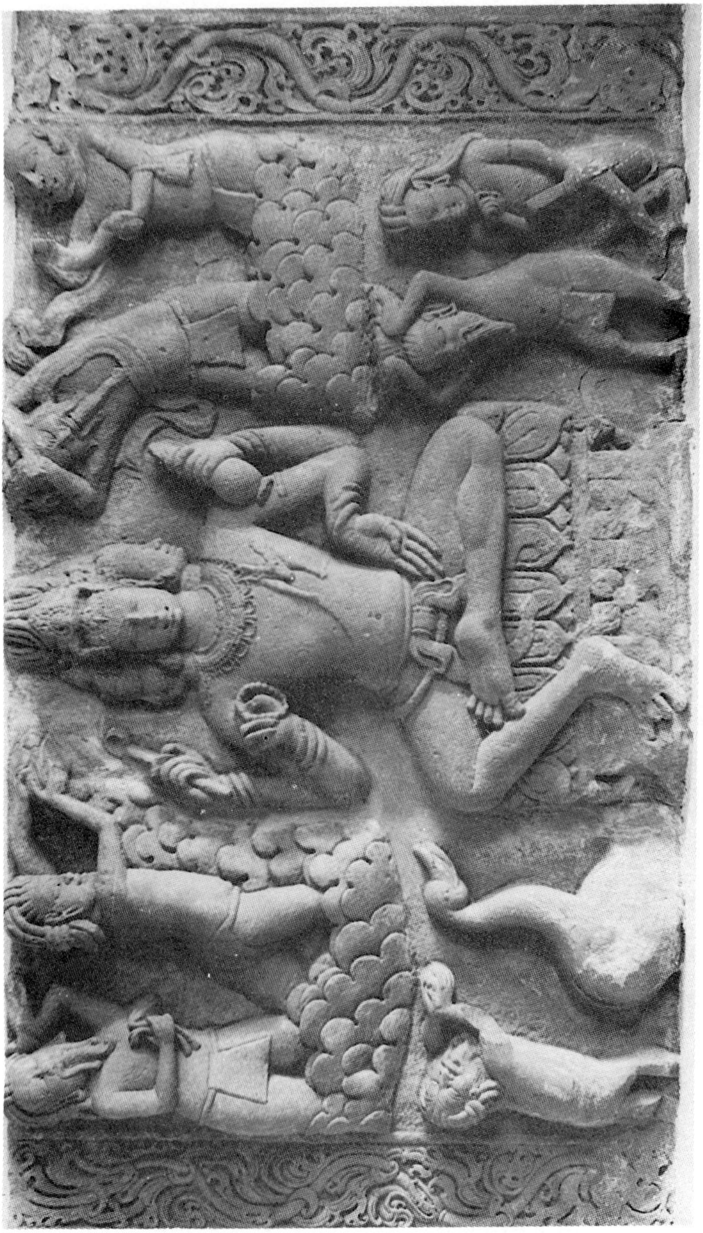

Plate 2: Brahmā Sitting on Lotus, Aihole, Kunti Temple, Chalukya, Circa 5th C. AD.

Prajāpati not only rested on the lotus leaf he also wanted to create. A passage in the *Taittirīya Āraṇyaka* mentions the desire for creation in Prajāpati:

> This world was water that was moving (*salilam*). He, Prajāpati, alone appeared on the lotus leaf. Within his mind originated a desire 'may I create this world.[17]

Prajāpati of the Vedic mythology, known as Brahmā in the Hindu mythology, is the Creator. Expressions like 'Prajāpati (Brahmā) appeared alone on the lotus leaf', incited sculptors to carve lotus as the seat of Brahmā or Prajāpati. Based on this Vedic story Brahmā is given the epithet 'self-born' (*svayambhū*) and lotus-born (*kamalayoni*) in Hindu mythology and he is always shown as sitting on an open lotus (Plate 2).

The word *salilam* connotes a special meaning with reference to the myths about cosmogony. In the Vedic Sanskrit *salilam* has been used as a qualifying word and there it means flowing, surging, unsteady. It points to the unstable, surging conditions of the primeval waters. Even in the later period *salilam* has been used to denote ruffled waters, wherever myths about cosmogony have been narrated, although in the classical Sanskrit it becomes a synonym of water, with a finger pointing to its unsteadiness.[18]

The rescue of the Earth from chaotic waters is first mentioned in the Brāhmaṇa period. The *Śatapatha Brāhmaṇa* says Prajāpati assuming the form of a boar raised the Earth from the cosmic waters and he was named as her Lord:

---

17 *āpo vā āsant salilam eva .sa prajāpatir ekaḥ puṣkaraparṇe samabhavat. tasyāntar manasi kāmaḥ samavartata idaṁ sṛjeyam iti.* TA 1.23.1
18 *Salila* is derived from the root *sal* - to go

> Then (earth) torn up by a boar (he takes), with, 'only thus large was this earth in the beginning' - for indeed only so large was this earth in the beginning, of the size of a span. A boar, called *emuṣa*, raised her up, and he was her lord Prajāpati.[19]

Though in this story *puṣkaraparṇa* as the support of the floating Earth is not mentioned *Taittirīya Brāhmaṇa* names lotus leaf as the support of the tossing Earth in its version of the same story:

> In the beginning this (world) was water, which was surging. Prajāpati grew tired by that. 'How can it be?' he said. He saw the lotus leaf standing. He thought 'indeed there must be something on which it rests'. Having taken the form of a boar, he dived near it. He obtained the Earth below. Having taken a fragment of it he came out. That he spread on the lotus leaf'[20]

'Prajāpati saw the lotus leaf standing' means, in the surging and unsteady cosmic waters, Prajāpati perceived the latent possibility of supporting the creation. He dived and brought out a fragment of the Earth, which he spread on the lotus leaf, which, in this context, signifies the cosmic waters with its potentiality of a firm support. Both in the *Śatapatha Brāhmaṇa* and *Taittirīya Brāhmaṇa* versions the pre-existence of Earth below the cosmic waters have been supposed. *Taittirīya Brahmaṇa* further says:

---

19 *atha varāhavihatam. īyatyagra āsīd īyatī ha vā iyam agre pṛthivyāsa prādesamātrī tām emuṣa iti varāho ujjaghāna so 'syāḥ patiḥ prajāpatiḥ.* SB 14.1.2.11. Translation by J. Eggeling, Satapatha Brahmana, Part V, p.451.

20 *āpo vā idam agre salilam āsīt tena prājapatir āsrāmyat. katham idaṁ syād iti. So 'paśyat puṣkaraparṇam tiṣṭhat. so 'manyat asti vai tad yasmin idam adhitiṣṭhatīti. sa varāharūpaṁ kṛtvopanyamajjat. sa pṛthivīm adha ārcchat.tasya upahatyodamajjat. tat puṣkaraparṇe 'prathayat.* TB 1.3.5-6.

> Prajāpati saw in the midst of the heaving sea the wide one (*urvī* = Earth), the stability of the moving one (*jagat* = world). That was indeed born of the support of the lotus[21].

The lotus (leaf) signifies the cosmic waters' role of support of the Earth by making it steady.

In the Vedic literature *puṣkaraparna* connotes the firmness in midst of unsteady water and thus becomes a symbol of stability. But in one place in the *Śatapatha Brāhmaṇa* this word does not symbolise anything but means simply a leaf of a lotus plant. There an (apparently) unstable helpless lotus leaf in water illustrates the condition of the tossing Earth in the cosmic waters[22] and for the first time in the Vedic literature the lotus (leaf) has been used as an *upamā*.

In the Vedic literature it is Prajāpati, who assumes the form of a boar and rescues the Earth from the chaotic cosmic waters but in the post-Vedic period Viṣṇu, the Lord of the universe dethrones Prajāpati. In the *Mārkaṇḍeya Purāṇa* (Chapter 39) it is said, after the end of the lotus aeon (*padma-kalpa*) Nārāyaṇa (i.e. Viṣṇu) awoke and came to know that the Earth was under the floodwater (*salilam*). He desired to rescue her. As in the previous aeons he had rescued the Earth having taken the shape of a fish (*matsya*) and a tortoise (*kūrma*). This time he entered the water taking the form of a boar (*varāha*) and established the Earth on the surging waters. Exceptions to this Viṣṇu-Boar-incarnation myth are found in the Liṅga Purāna, an ancient book belonging to the followers of Śiva and in the great epic *Rāmāyaṇa*[23]. Both the books repeat the Vedic theory and say, the self-born Brahmā, a later name of Prajāpati, assumed the form of a boar and rescued the Earth.

---

21 *yat paryapaśyaj sarirasya madhye / urvīm apaśyaj jagataḥ pratiṣṭhām/ tat puṣkarasyāyatanād hi jātam ...//*TB 1.2.1.4.*sarira* and *salila* are synonyms as interchange of *r*.and *l* is quite common. Cf. Monier-Williams, Sans.-Eng. Dictionary.

22 *heyam pṛthivyalelayad yathā puṣkaraparnam* SB 2.1.1.8.

23 Rāmāyaṇa 2.110.3-4.

In the sculpture of Boar-incarnation (Plate 3) the boar holds a club in one of his right hands. The goddess Earth is placed on his left shoulder. In one of his left hands he holds a conch shell, the other weapon in his other left hand is probably a wheel (*cakra*). These three weapons are associated with Lord Viṣṇu. The serpent-king Śeṣanāga holds a lotus-umbrella over Viṣṇu's head, while his left foot rests on a lotus flower held by Śeṣanāga's consort. Śeṣanāga, the serpent-king, symbolises the heaving cosmic waters and the lotus under the boar's foot symbolises the Vedic conception of cosmic waters' potential energy of supporting the creation.

2.3 The Sun and Heaven

Ṛgvedic poets expressed the various forms of Agni as his various births. The Sun in heaven, the thunder in atmosphere and the fire on this earth are forms of Agni. The *Ṛg-Veda* calls Agni 'the child of heaven' (*divoḥ śiśum* – RV 4.15.6) by which the sun is meant. As the sun in heaven and as fire on the earth Agni is also called *dvijanman,* having two births. This is based on the Vedic notion that the universe is divided in two divisions, heaven and earth. *Śatapatha Brāhmaṇa* specifies Agni as the lotus of this earth and the sun of the heaven.[24] *Puṣkara,* the sire of Agni, which represents water in the creation myths, has been identified with the heaven[25]. Undoubtedly in these two hymns the Sun, a form of Agni or Fire, is meant. *Puṣkara* as the birthplace of Agni-Sun, represents the heaven also as according to the notions prevailing in the Vedic times there was a big ocean in the heaven. A hymn in the *Ṛg-Veda* says that 'the sun deposits the darkness like a skin within the waters'.[26] This also corroborates the view that the heaven was thought as a big ocean (apparently because of the blue colour of both heaven (read sky) and ocean). The *Śatapatha Brāhmaṇa* explains this camouflaged identification of the lotus and heaven,

---

24 See footnote 34.

25 *enaṁ dyaur janayat suretaḥ* - RV 10.45.8

26 *raśmayaḥ sūryasya carmevāvādhus tamo apsu antaḥ.* RV 4.13.4.

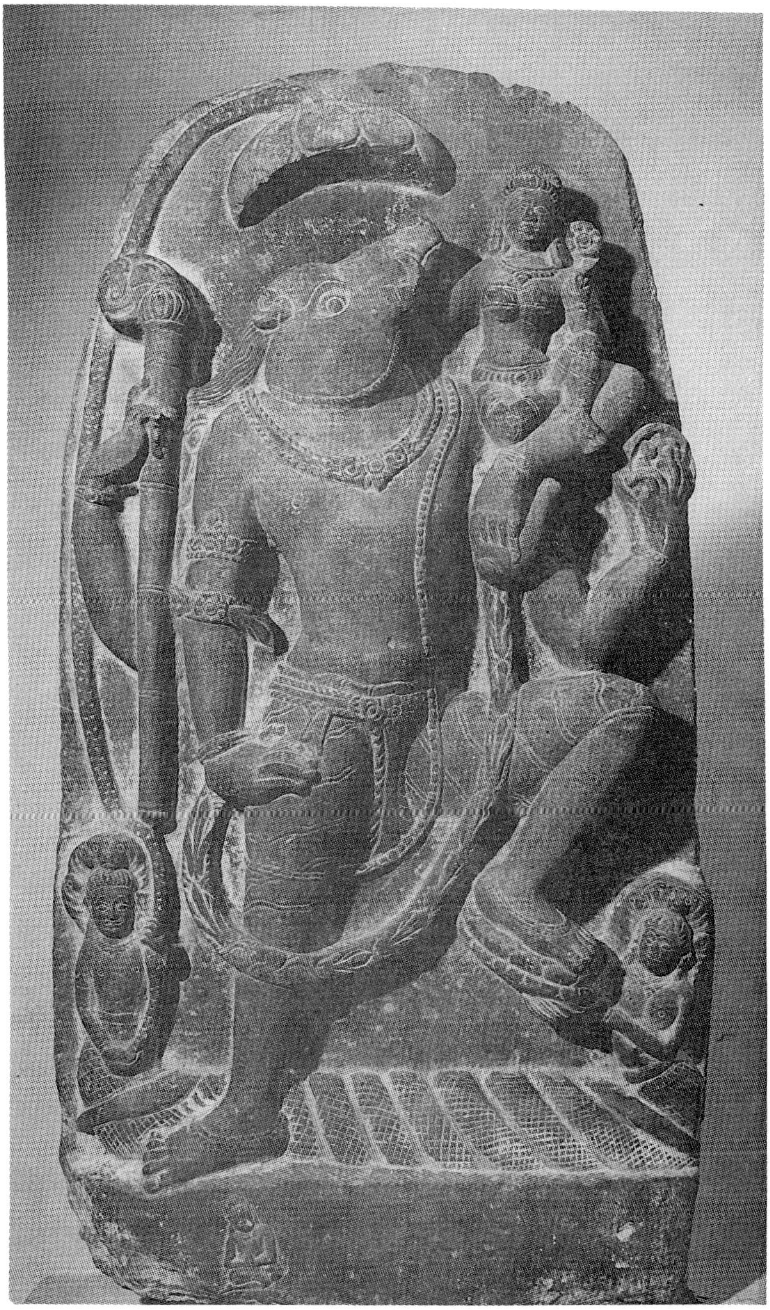

Plate 3: Boar-incarnation of Viṣṇu, 10th C. AD., Pala style

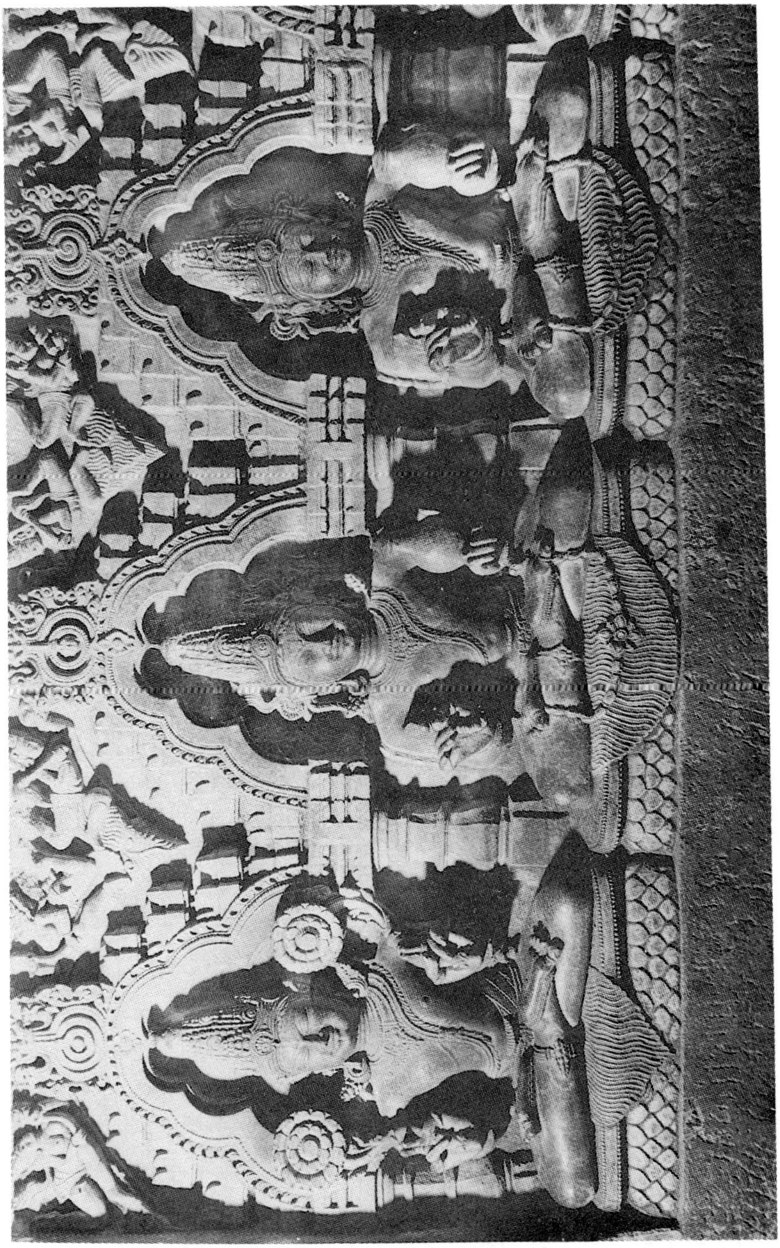

Plate 4: Navagraha Slab (L. to R.) Sūrya, Soma and Maṅgala, Konarak, 13th C. AD.

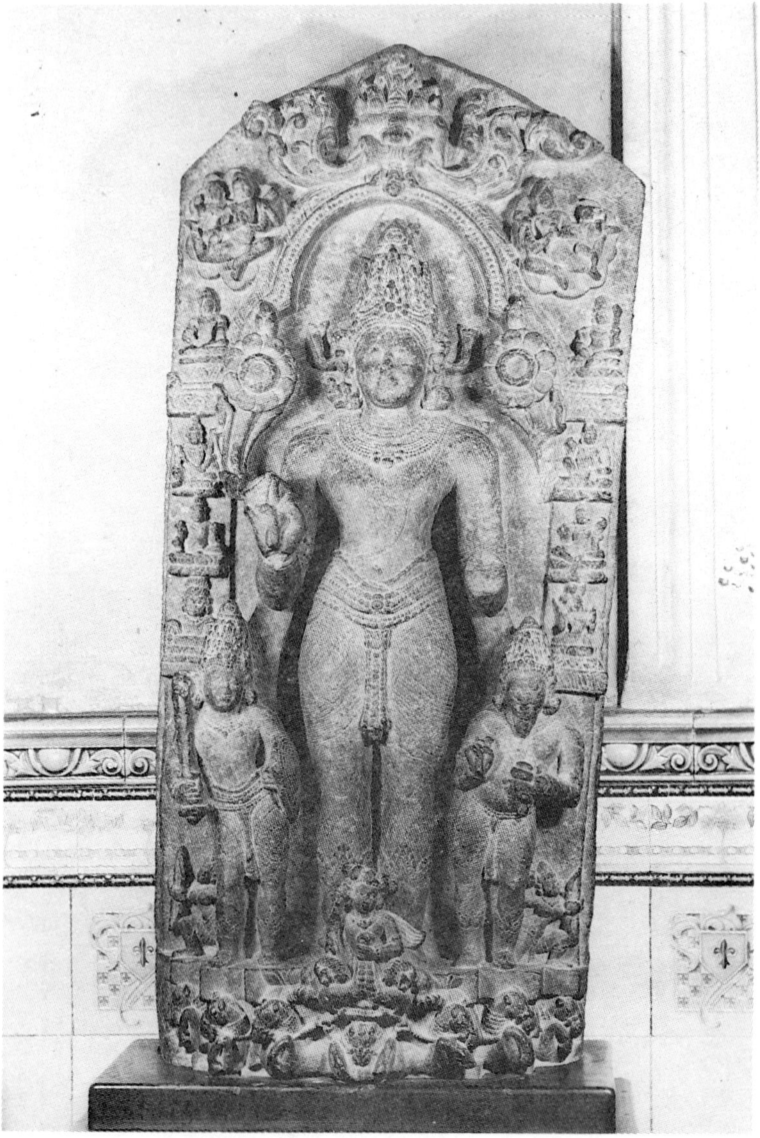

Plate 5: Sūrya or the Sun God standing on the lotus, 10th C. AD., Nandigram, Dt. Hoogly..

mentioned in the *Ṛg-Veda* and says: "The lotus leaf (*puṣkara-parṇa*) is heaven. Truly water is heaven. The lotus leaf is water."[27]. Furthermore, a devotee prays to the Sun and expresses his wish thus: "You are the lotus (*puṇḍarīka*) of heaven's quarters. May I be one (*puṇḍarīka*) among people."[28]

To the Vedic people lotus was a symbol of power, as the various myths about lotus show[29], and hence the wish. In this hymn it is noteworthy that for lotus *puṇḍarīka* and not *puṣkara* has been used, as this flower does not play the role of a support. Whereas, in the case of heaven the lotus is supposed to be the sire of Agni-Sun, and there the word *puṣkara* has been used.

In association with Sūrya (Sun) the lotus symbolises heaven – the sire of Sun god (Plates 4,5).

2.4 Aśvinā

The twin gods Aśvinā hold an important place in the Vedic mythology. There is a myth about the origin of their name. It is said they are born of Sūrya (the Sun) and a nymph, who transformed herself into a mare (*aśva*). Hence they are called Aśvinā (Horsemen).[30] Another version says they are sons of Vivasvant (a synonym of the sun) and Saraṇyū, daughter of Tvaṣṭṛ, the artificer among the gods. Two of the epithets of the Asvinā are *dasra* (miracle-worker) and *nāsatya* (true). In the hymns in the *Ṛg-Veda* they have been requested to ward off languor and diseases and bring wealth to mortals. They are divine physicians healing diseases with their remedies, restoring sight, curing the sick and the maimed. Several legends are mentioned about those whom they restored to youth and cured of various defects. The name most often mentioned is that of Bhujyu whom they saved from the ocean in a ship.[31] As

---

27 *dyauḥ puṣkaraparṇam āpo vai dyaur āpaḥ puṣkaraparṇam* – SB 6.4.1.9

28 *diśām ekaṁ puṇḍarīkam asy ahaṃ manuṣyānām ekaṃ puṇḍarīkaṁ bhūyāsam* SB 14.9.3.14

29 See p. 41ff.

30 Cf. Veronica Ions, *Indische Mythologie*, p. 23.

31 Macdonell, *A Vedic Reader*, p. 129.

possessors of *dasra,* i.e. magical power, they performed various miracles. One of the miraculous acts is the deliverance of the sage Cyavāna from old age.[32] The story of Cyavāna, referred to in the *Ṛg-Veda*, is mentioned in the later literature. In short the story runs thus. Immortal Cyavāna became very old, frail and ugly. His body and face were full of wrinkles. One day some boys seeing ugly Cyavāna threw stones at him, which angered the sage very much. Fearing repercussion from the sage the father of one of the boys gave him his daughter in marriage. Once the Aśvinā came to visit the hermitage of the sage. There they saw the old and wrinkle-faced Cyavāna. They took pity on the young and beautiful wife of the sage and rejuvenated him[33].

Another epithet of Aśvinā is "the lotus-garlanded ones" (*puṣkarasrajau* - RV 10.184.2) and they have been praised for their beauty. But the significance of lotus as an aid to personal adornment does not end here in the case of the twin gods. 'Agni is the lotus of this earth, and the sun of that yonder sky and the two Aśvinā possess everything here, as they wear lotus garlands'[34] says *Śatapatha Brāhmaṇa*. Hence it can be said that the lotus garlands of the two Aśvinā are symbols of their power.

2.5 Vasiṣṭha

Vasiṣṭha is one of the composers of the hymns of the *Ṛg-Veda* and many hymns have been attributed to him. It is said Varuṇa inspired him to compose hymns.[35] That may be the reason that Varuṇa along with his partner Mitra are supposed to be Vasiṣṭha's father. As the son of Mitra and Varuṇa he was received on the *puṣkara*, informs a hymn in the *Ṛg-Veda*:

---

32 'Ye two released Cyavāna from old age, ye brought a swift horse to Pedu, ye rescued Atri from distress and darkness; ye placed Jāhuṣa in freedom.' RV 7.71.5. Translation by A.A. Macdonell, *Vedic Reader*, p. 133.

33 See Veronica Ions, *Indische Mythologie*, p. 23.

34 *yad aśvinau itīme ha vai dyāvāpṛthivī pratyakṣam aśvinau ime hīdam sarvam aśnuvātām puṣkarasrajau iti agnir evasyai puṣkaram ādityo amuṣyai* SB 4.1.5.16

35 See Monier-Williams, *Sans.-Eng. Dictionary*

> And you, Vasiṣṭha, are the son of Mitra and Varuṇa. You are born out of mere thought of Urvaśī. O High Priest, you, the spilled drops (*drapsaṁ skannam*) were received by all the gods on the lotus under divine spell.[36]

Varuṇa is one of the oldest Vedic gods. In the *Ṛg-Veda* Varuṇa is primarily the guardian deity of *ṛta* or the cosmic order. He hates falsehood and transgression of law and as a punishment he inflicts the transgressor with dropsy. He is often invoked in the hymns along with his associate Mitra. The duo Mitrā-Varuṇā has practically the same attributes also. They possess *māyā* or occult power, by which 'they send dawns, make the sun traverse the sky and obscure it with clouds and rain'"[37]. Mitrā –Varuṇā have also been invoked to bestow rain to uphold *ṛta* or cosmic order and the pair is called *sindhupati* (Lords of rivers or oceans – RV 7.64.2), as without rain there can neither be rivers nor oceans. In later mythology this attribute of Varuṇa gains prominence and he becomes the god of oceans. In this hymn Varuṇa's as well as Mitra's association with water is implied and the word *puṣkara* symbolises the Ṛgvedic expression of the latent firmness in water, on which Vasiṣṭha was received.

Vasiṣṭha's association with Mitra-Varuṇa might have its origin in the rivalry between the seers Vasiṣṭha and Viśvāmitra, another composer of Ṛgvedic verses. Viśvāmitra originally belonged to the warrior (*kṣatrīya*) caste and by intense austerities had elevated himself to the *brāhmaṇa* caste (*Manu* 7.42). Vasiṣṭha belonged to the *brāhmaṇa* caste by birth[38]. Both were priests in the service of King Sudas and thus developed

---

36 *utāsi mitrā-varuṇā vasiṣṭhorvaśyā brahman manaso 'dhi jātāḥ / drapsaṁ skannaṁ brahmaṇā daivyena viśve devāḥ puṣkare tv ādadantaḥ //* RV 7.33.11 Rendered into English from K.F. Geldner's German translation in *Der Rigveda*.

37 A.A. Macdonell, *A Vedic Reader*, p.118.

38 Cf. Monier-Williams, *Sans.-Eng. Dictionary* under *vasiṣṭha*. Mahabharat 164-165, Rāmāyaṇa 1.51-56.

rivalry. Vasiṣṭha by associating himself with Mitrā-Varuṇā and the celestial beauty Urvaśī, perhaps wanted to prove his divine origin and thus gain dominance over his rival.

What is *drapsaṁ skannam*? Monier-Williams and Grassmann [39] both say *drapsa* is 'semen' and *skanna* means 'fallen, sprinkled'. In the post-Vedic period an explanation was found unravelling the mystery of Vasiṣṭha's birth. Rāmāyaṇa narrates the story thus:

> Once Urvaśī came for water sports along with other celestial maids *(apsarās)*. Varuṇa saw the beautiful Urvaśī, fell in love instantly and selected her for cohabitation. Though Urvaśī felt attracted to Varuṇa but rejected him on the ground that Mitra had already selected her. Varuṇa did not want to enjoy her against her wishes and poured forth his seminal fluid in a jar and thus satisfied went away. Urvaśī had already received Mitra's virility, with that combined the virility of Varuṇa. Thus after some time Vasiṣṭha was born having two fathers – Mitra and Varuṇa and he is called Maitrā-Varuṇi (son of Mitra and Varuṇa)[40].

Lotus in association with the sage Vasiṣṭha is a symbol of water, on which the gods received him.

2.6 World-Wheel

The Agni-lotus connection again emerges in conjunction with the world-wheel. Agni is the nave of movable and immovable worlds (*viśvasya nābhihm carato dhruvasya*) and also the nave of immortality (*amṛtasya nābhim*) says the *Ṛg-Veda* in the hymns 10.5.3 and 3.17.4 respectively. In another hymn it is said: 'All beings are placed in this never-ageing (*ajara*), incomparable wheel'[41]. In some Vedic verses lotus

---

39 *Sanskrit-English Dictionary* and Wörterbuch zum Rigveda.

40 Rāmāyaṇa 7.56,57.

41 *tri-nābhi-cakram ajaram anarvam/*
yatremā viśvā bhuvanādhitasthuḥ // RV 1.164.2. RV 1.164.11,13 say that this (world-)wheel supports all the worlds and it is rotating.

replaces Agni as the nave, since lotus is the birthplace and support of Agni:

> Where gods and human beings are fixed like spikes around a nave, oh Flower of waters, I ask thee, where they are set into motion by supernatural power'[42]

The world-wheel is *ajara,* i.e. non-aging. In other words world-wheel will never die which is tantamount to *amṛta* (immortal). It means that Agni is the nave of this *amṛta* or *ajara* world-wheel that comprises of movable and immovable worlds. This embraces also gods who have been counted as one of the constituents along with human beings rotating around the nave. In the Atharvavedic verse 'flower of water' or lotus has been named as the nave of the world-wheel instead of Agni, as the lotus is the birthplace as well as the support of Agni.

As the nave of the world-wheel lotus is a symbol of immortality.

The lotus ceiling from Konarak is carved like a wheel (Plate 6). The figure of a deity in the nave of the wheel is surrounded by two rows of lotus petals. Figures, some of which are of human beings and some might be of deities, are carved on the second row of petals.

2.7 Womb

The birth of Agni branched out into various symbols and conceptions associated with the lotus and in this process it became a symbol of generative force also. This leads to its identification with womb in the books, which are later to the *Ṛg-Veda*[43]. But from a verse from the *Ṛg-Veda* it seems that the association of the lotus and womb was lurking in a corner of the poet's mind also though it was not said expressly as in the later period. The verse wishes:

---

42 *yatra devās ca manuṣyās cārā nābhāviva sritāh / apām tvāṁ puṣpaṁ pṛcchāmi yatra tan māyayā hitam //* AV 10.8.34.

43 Lotus has been identified with womb in TS 5.2.6.5; VS 11.29, 13.2; SB 6.4.1.7, 6.4.3.6, 7.4.1.7, 8.3.1.11, 8.6.3.7.

> As the wind stirs the lotus pond in all directions, similarly your foetus should agitate itself; it should come out after ten months.[44]

In the *Taittirīya Saṁhitā* it is said in clear terms:

> You are the back of waters and he (one who offers) takes the lotus leaf. This is indeed the back of waters, which is the lotus leaf. He takes, indeed with its (own) form and puts together with lotus leaf. That lotus leaf is the womb for Agni. He indeed puts Agni together with the womb.[45]

Ultimately in the Puranic period the womb was imagined as shaped like a lotus (*padmavad garbhāśayaḥ* – *Agni Purāṇa* 370). In the wedding hymn in the *Ṛg-Veda* (10.85) the twin gods Asvinā (along with other gods) are entreated to bestow fertility on the bride. Perhaps the association of the lotus and womb is one of the reasons to invoke Asvinā, the lotus-garlanded ones.

Lotus, a symbol of womb, is also hinted at in a story in the *Nidānkathā*, a commentary on the *Jātaka* stories. According to it Queen Māyā, the mother of prince Siddhārtha had a dream before her conception that a white elephant holding a white lotus in his trunk had entered her womb. After that dream prince Siddhārtha was born. In this story the lotus stands as a symbol of womb pointing to the happening that she would conceive. Secondly, the lotus as a symbol of purity in the Buddhist period indicates that her child would be the purest among human beings. This dream of Queen Māyā, the mother of Siddhārtha, has been frozen on stone in the stupa of Bharhut by one of the numerous unknown artists (Plate 7) but the lotus in the trunk of the elephant is not there.

---

44 *yathā vātaḥ puṣkariṇiṁ samiṅgayati sarvataḥ/ evā te garbhaḥ ejatu niraitu daśamāsyaḥ //* RV 5.78.7.

45 *apāṁ pṛṣṭham asti puskara-parnam āharaty apāṁ vā etat pṛṣṭhaṁ yat puṣ karaparṇaṁ rupeṇaiva enad āharati puṣkaraparnena saṁbharati yonir vā agneḥ puṣkaraparṇam sayonim evāgniṁ saṁbharati.* TS 5.2.4.1-2.

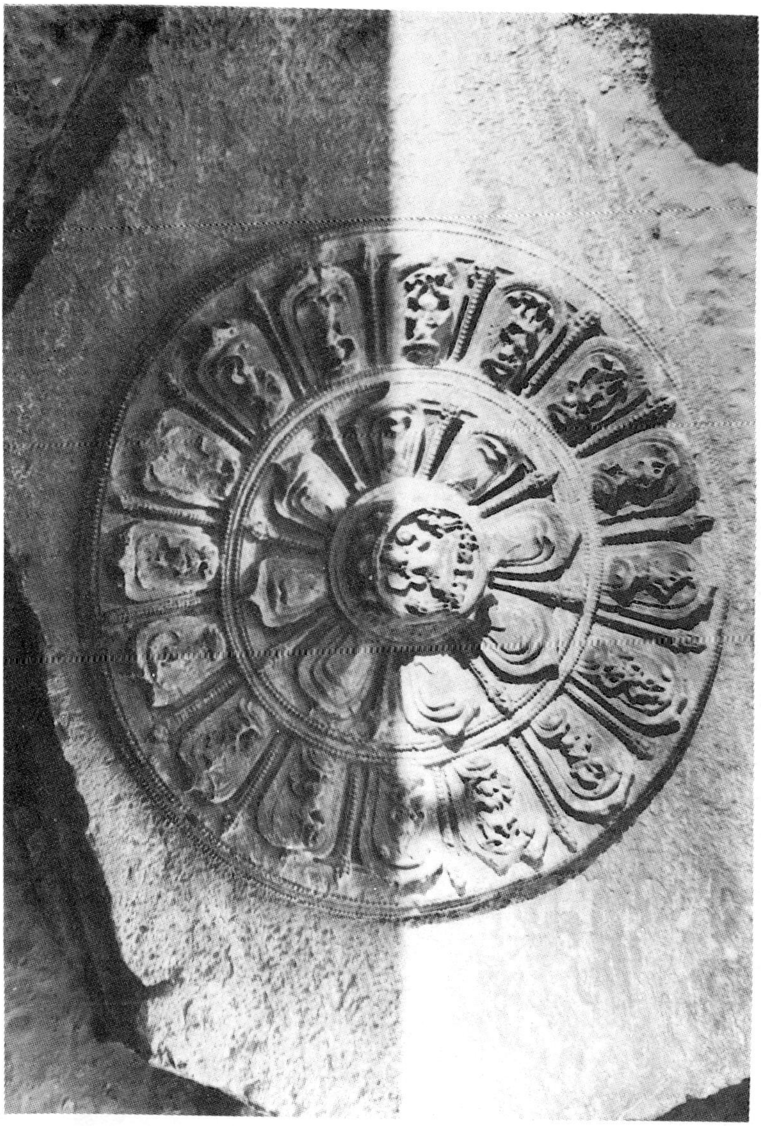

Plate 6: Lotus-ceiling, Konarak, 13th C. AD.

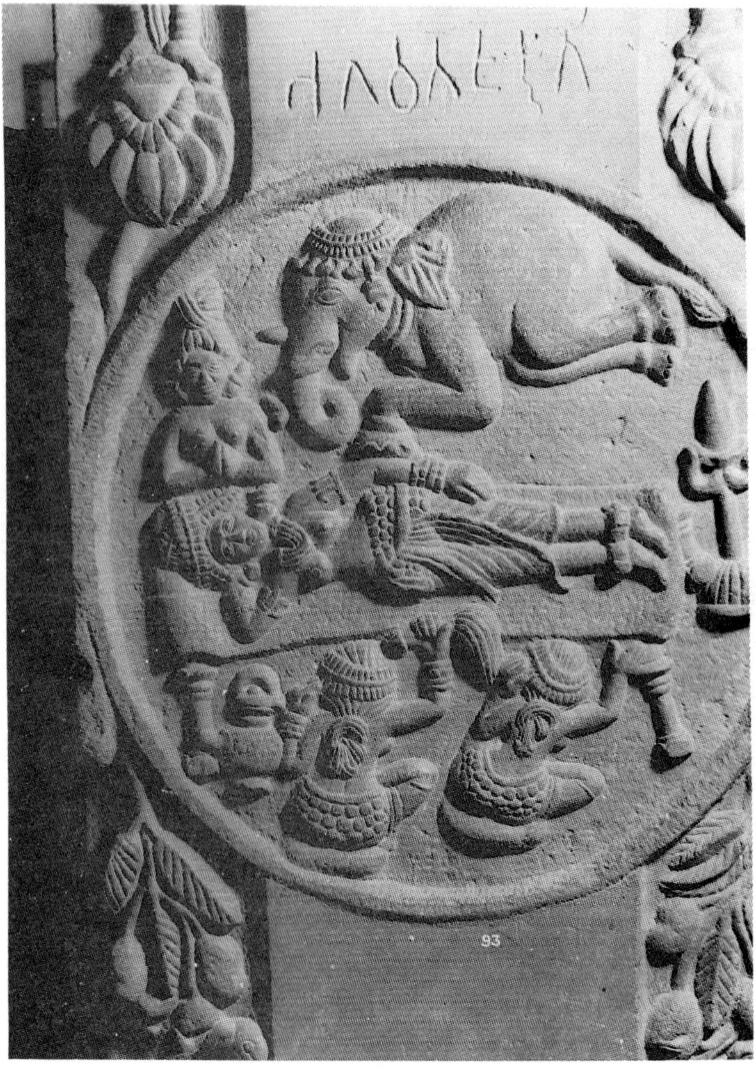

Plate 7: Dream of Māyā, Bharhut, 2nd, C. BC.

2.8 Immortality

The lotus, the birthplace of Agni and identified with the womb, is also seen as a support of immortal beings. In other words, immortal beings are born on the lotus – the immortal element. In a verse in the *Atharva-Veda* this idea is elaborated:

> *Viṣṭārin*[46] is the best carrier of sacrifices. Having cooked the *viṣṭārin* the one who offers has entered the heaven. The bulb-bearing lotus spreads all over the pond as also the lotus-stalk, the root and the lotus-fibre. Let all these streams come to thee, and complete lotus ponds, swelling with honey let approach thee in the heavenly world[47].

'Let complete lotus ponds approach thee' is an indirect reference to immortality attached to the lotus. The *Śatapata Brāhmaṇa* says, the lotus is the immortal element itself:

> And the immortal element, which is flame that is glowing, is the lotus leaf. Having laid down that which is lotus leaf he (one, who offers) piles up fire (constructs a fire altar). On that he prepares an immortal existence for himself consisting of *ṛk*, *yajus* and *sāman*. He becomes immortal[48].

This passage from the *Śatapatha Brāhmaṇa* serves as an exposition of the Atharvavedic idea, where the poet expresses it in a more significant and mysterious language, 'let complete lotus ponds approach thee', which means, let you be born on the lotus, i.e. the immortal element

---

46 *Viṣṭārin* is a kind of offering for gods.

47 *eṣa yajñānām vitato vahiṣṭho viṣṭāriṇam paktvā divam āviveśa/*
āṇḍikaṁ kumudam santanoti bisam śālukam śaphako mulāli//
etastvā dhārā upayantu sarvāḥ svarge loke madhumatpinvamānā/
upa tvā tiṣṭhantu puṣkariṇīḥ samantāḥ// AV 4.34.5.

48 *athaitad amṛtaṁ yat etad arcir dīpyata idam tat puṣkaraparṇam tad yat puṣkaraparṇam upadhāyāgniṁ cinoty etasmin evaitad amṛta ṛṇmayaṁ yajurmayaṁ sāmamayam ātmānaṁ saṁskurute so 'mṛto bhavati.* – SB 10.5.1.5
In the *Jaminīya Upaniṣad Brāhmaṇa* (4.3) a significant appellation has been given to lotuses by naming them 'flowers of immortality' (*amṛtasya puṣpāṇi*).

The idea of birth on lotus finds its way also in the Buddhist texts. In the *Jātaka* tales and *Apadāna*, the books of popular Buddhism, births on lotus flowers as a result of being virtuous have been narrated. The nun Uppalavaṇṇā[49] was conceived inside a lotus as a result of offering fried corns covered with lotus to a *Paccekabuddha* (one who is enlightened but keeps the knowledge to himself and does not share with others.)

A contrast can be marked about lotus-birth on account of philosophical idea on one hand and folk belief on the other. In the Vedic literature lotus symbolizes immortality. The idea of becoming immortal has been expressed by saying that immortal personages will be born on the lotus. Here not an actual birth on a lotus flower in the nature is meant but immortality. Whereas in the Pāli Canonical texts a natural flower is meant and it does not signify anything further. Neither has it any connection with immortality, since in the stories of *Therī Apadāna* and the *Jātaka* the persons, born inside a lotus were mortals and hence died after the run of life was over. A Buddhist text of a much later period - *Sukhāvatī-Vyūha* - repeats the Vedic conception of lotus birth of meritorious persons in the heaven. *Sukhāvāti-Vyūha* is the paradise of Amitābha Buddha of the Mahāyana school of thought. According to this text the chosen ones are born on lotuses in the paradise of Amitabha Buddha.[50]

The Buddhist doctrine of karma says deeds bear their fruits through the medium of lust or desire. As soon as the lust or desire ceases, karma is annihilated, which is the ultimate goal of a disciple. He is not born again. The deeds, good and

---

49 *Cf. disvā paccekasambuddhaṃ pañcalājasatān ahaṃ/*
datvā paduma-channāni pañcaputtasatān ahaṁ//56//
patthayiṁ tesu patthesu madhuṁ datvā sayabhuno/
tato cutā araññehaṁ ajāyiṁ padumodare//57// *Therī Apadāna* 19.
'Seeing the Paccekabuddha, I having given five hundred fried corn covered with lotuses and honey in pots to the Self-born, prayed for five hundred sons. Seperated from there (that life) I was born in the womb of a lotus in the woods.' (Tr., Pali Text Society).

50 S. Morenz and J. Schubert, Der Gott auf der Blume, p.132.

bad, condition the next birth, which is illustrated by folk-tales and beliefs, thus making the doctrine less enigmatic for the laity. The folk believed in these tales and were encouraged to perform virtuous deeds. Offering flowers as a mark of respect was one of these. *Vimānavatthu*, another book of popular tales, narrates a tale of four ladies, who offered flowers including lotuses to monks begging for alms. As a result of this appreciable deed they were born in the kingdom of gods (*Vimānavatthu* 45.5). To bar anybody from worshipping the Buddha was considered a sin. A man was born in the 'world of dead' (*pretaloka*), because he barred his wife and daughter-in-law from offering lotus to a stupa.[51] This punishment was the result of an evil karma.

The lotus flower is connected with the Buddha's nativity[52] and offering it to a Paccekabuddha, or to a stupa signifies the respect to the Buddha himself.

2.9 Myths About Lotus

The association of lotus with metaphysical ideas such as cosmogony gives rise to myths about its mysterious origin in the later Vedic period. These myths are based on the different natural characteristics of this aquatic plant, which allowed different symbolical meanings to be ascribed to it. One such myth ascribes strength or power to the lotuses, which these gained from heavenly bodies. Heavenly bodies in turn obtained the power from the mighty demon Vṛtra. What else can be a better proof of the power of the lotuses than to associate these with Vṛtra. A myth about the origin of lotuses alludes to the fight between Indra, the king of gods and his rival Vṛtra. In the Vedic mythology the dark side of the nature, particularly drought and darkness, is personified as the demon Vṛtra. Indra wages war against him and kills him with his weapon thunderbolt (*vajra*), which is lightning. Indra is also invoked to dispel darkness and to win light or the sun. Indra slays Vṛtra, releases water from the clouds and places the sun in the heaven

51 *Petavatthu* 3.10.5.
52 See p. 36.

for the benefit of human beings. Alluding to this fight the *Maitrāyaṇī Saṁhita*, a recension of *Black Yajur-Veda*, says:

> Indra slew Vṛtra. These two obtained his forms; she (earth obtained) the variegated forms and he (heaven) the heavenly bodies. Through the down-shining of heavenly bodies the lotus (*puṇḍarīka*) springs up. It is the form of power.[53]

The *Pañchaviṁśa Brāhmaṇa* also repeats the same story with minor variation:

> Indra slew Vṛtra (when) she (earth) obtained his variegated forms, (and) that (heaven) the appearances. Through the down-shining of heavenly bodies the lotus (*puṇḍarīka*) is born. In that, he (the sacrificer) fastens a lotus-garland (*puṣkarasrajam*), he fastens on himself the appearance of Vṛtra, the power.[54]

The *Śatapatha Brāhmaṇa* without naming Vṛtra or his power says, lotuses (*puṇḍarīka*) are 'appearances of heaven; appearances of heavenly bodies'.[55] It is noteworthy, that in these texts another name for lotus, *puṇḍarīka,* has been used and often these two nomenclatures - *puṣkara* and *puṇḍarīka*– interchange their places.

The sun, moon and stars belong to the heavenly bodies. In these texts both *puṣkara* and *puṇḍarīka* stand for lotus in general, i.e. day lotus as well as night water lilies. The natural characteristic of the flowers of the family *Nymphaeaceae* is that its flowers blossom at different times of the day and night.[56] This fact has been wrapped in mystery in these passages. Moreover, the heavenly bodies, viz., the sun, moon and stars

---

53 *indro vai vṛtram ahaṁs. tasyeme rūpāṇy upaitām.citrāṇyam nakṣatrāni asau. nakṣatrāṇām vāvakaśe puṇḍarīkaṁ jāyate. kṣatrasya vā etad rūpam.* MS 4.4.7

54 *indro vai vṛtram ahaṁs. tasyemaṃ citrāny upaid. rūpany asau. nakṣatrāṇām avakāśena puṇḍarīkan jāyate. yat puṣkasrajam pratimuñcate.* PB 18.9.6

55 *yāni puṇḍarīkāni tāni divo rūpam tāni nakṣatrāṇāṁ rūpam.* SB 5.4.5.14.

56 See p. 84.

are, as the passages say, a form of *Vṛtra,* and therefore very powerful. By the light of the heavenly bodies lotuses are born. This alludes to the power associated with these flowers and to emphasise the power of the lotuses these are brought in connection with Vṛtra. The *Taittirīya Saṁhitā* corroborates the strength of this flower when it says, 'growing mighty like the lotus flower, do thou extend in width with the measure of heaven.'[57] In this passage the word *puṣkara* and not *puṇḍarīka* has been used.

The *Śatapatha Brāhmaṇa* (7.4.1.13) speculates on the etymology of the word *puṣkara* and we have another story about its origin also woven round the fight of the two mighty rivals:

> Once Indra, having smitten the demon Vṛtra, thought, the latter had not died and sought asylum in the waters. The waters gathered up their essence (*rasaḥ*) and made a stronghold for Indra. *Puḥ* means 'stronghold' and *kar* means 'made'. Therefore, *puṣkara* represents the stronghold of Indra. It has been named so as the gods love mystical names.

There are two reasons for defining lotus as the essence of water: (i) as a refuge for Indra, the king of gods, it was supposed to be the best and (ii) as a stronghold in the midst of unstable waters it was supposed to be made of the best materials.

The best element of any object is considered to be its *rasaḥ* (essence). Lord Kṛṣṇa says in the *Gītā*: 'I am the *rasaḥ* in the waters'.[58] The lotus, though an offspring of mud and water[59], does not resemble its parents, suggesting that it is born of their best elements. *Rasaḥ,* which is *soma* or elixir (*amṛta*) of life itself, nourishes creatures[60]. The lotus is the embodiment

---

57 *vardhamānam maha ā ca puṣkaram divo mātrayā variṇā pṛthasva.* TS 4.2.8.2.

58 *raso'ham apsu. Gita* 7.8.

59 The words *pañkaja, pañkeruha* (mud-born), *saroja, sarasīja* (water-born) are synonyms of lotus and points to its origin.

60 Cf. F.D.K. Bosch, *The Golden Germ*, pp.59-60.

of that nourishment or elixir of life. The explanation of the word *puṣkara* given in the *Nirukta,* an ancient text on etymology belonging to the *Vedāṅga* literature, also corroborates the notion about the lotus exemplifying its role as a support. Yāska (ca. 700 B.C.), the author of *Nirukta* says, 'it nourishes the living beings' (*poṣati bhūtāni*) hence it is called *puṣkara*.

Not only with Vṛtra lotus is also brought in connection with the creative energy of Varuṇa and the Aṅgirasas to emphasise the supernatural strength of this highly esteemed flower. In the *Pañcaviṁśa Brāhmaṇa* it is said:

> The lustre of Varuṇa departed as he was consecrated. It fell into three parts. One third became Bhṛgu (the seer), one- third *śrāyantīya (sāman)* and one third entered the water... He who puts on a lotus garland, by him that virility is obtained having reached it (virility).[61].

In the Vedic literature Varuṇa is praised as the universal monarch and is called *kṣatriya*[62]. Hence in the *rājasūya*-sacrifice the king is associated with Varuṇa. Varuṇa is also associated with water[63]. Lotus, the symbol of water, is the symbol of the lustre of Varuṇa, which had entered water. The king obtains that lustre by putting on a lotus wreath.

The *Maitrāyaṇī Saṁhitā* repeats the same myth and reports on the loss of Varuṇa's procreative energy (not lustre) but nothing on lotus, although one third of his energy entered Sarasvati, the river:

> The virility of Varuṇa departed as he was sprinkled (with water). It split into three parts. One third became *Bhṛgu,* one third became

61 *varuṇasya vai suṣuvāṇasya bhargo 'pākrāmat. a tredhāpatad bhṛgustṛitīyam abhvac chrāyantīyaṁ tṛtīyam āpas tṛtīyam prāviśad ...yat puṣkarasrajam pratimuñcate tenaiva tad indriyam vīryam āptvāvarundhe.* PB 18.9.1-2

62 See A.A. Macdonell, *Vedic Mythology*, p. 24

63 See p. 33-34.

śrāyantīya and one third entered Sarasvatī. Therefore *hotā* belongs to *bhārgava* (family),[64] *śrāyantīya* is *brahma*-chant and Sarasvatī is water.

The *Taittirīya Brāhmaṇa* connects the origin of the lotus with the heat and consecration of the Aṅgirasas, which entered water. Aṅgirasas means descendants of Aṅgiras, another name of Agni (RV 1.1.6; 5.11.6 etc.) The identification of Agni with Angiras may be because both execute the same function. Both are intermediaries between gods and human beings. *Taittirīya Brāhmaṇa* says:

> The Aṅgirasas while going to the region of heaven let enter their consecration (*dikṣā*) and heat (*tapas*) into water. That became the lotus (*puṇḍarīka*)[65].

Whether 'virility' (*indriyam vīryam*) of the *Maitrāyiṇī Saṁhitā* or 'lustre' (*bhargo*) of the *Pañchaviṁśa Brāhmaṇa* or 'consecration and heat' (*dikṣā-tapasī*) of the *Taittirīya Brāhmaṇa* the inherent meaning of these words is creative energy. The word, *tapas* has been derived from the root *tap* (to heat). Radhakrishnan writes: "*Tapas* is just `rushing forth', the spontaneous `outgrowth', the projection of beings into existence, the energising impulse, the innate spiritual fervour of the Absolute"[66]. *Tapas* is one of the four constituents which created. The other three constituents are time (*saṁvatsara*), desire (*kāma*) and intelligence (*puruṣa*) according to the Indian metaphysical conceptions[67]. *Tapas* started the whole process says the *Ṛg-Veda* in one of its metaphysical hymns on creation:

---

64 *varunasya vā abhiṣicyamānasya indriyaṁ vīryam apākrāmat.tad tredhābhavat. bhṛgustṛtiyam abhavat śrāyantīyaṁ tṛtiyaṃ sarasvatīṃ tṛtiyaṃ prāviśad.yad bhārgavo hotā bhavati śrāyantiyaṁ brahmasāmam sarasvatīr āpaḥ.* MS 4.3.9

65 *aṅgirasaḥ suvargaṃ lokaṁ yantaḥ apsu dīkṣātapasī prāveśayan. tat puṇḍarīkam abhavat.* TB 1.8.2.1.

66 S. Radhakrishnan, *Indian Philosophy*, Part 1, p. 102.

67 *Ibid* p.99.

> In the beginning darkness was hidden by darkness: All this was indistinguishable surging water (*salilam*). When void was covered with void, that One was born through the power of (creative) energy[68].

The primeval waters were surging, heaving, moving due to the thrust of energy inside it and that inner force started the creation. Regarding *tapas* and *salilam* the *Atharva-Veda* in its Creation Hymn says:

> The great Yakṣa, full of creative energy (*tapas*) lay on the back of heaving waters (*salilam*). On him gods are set like branches of a tree[69].

The Great Yakṣa (*mahadyakṣa*) is Varuṇa, who is associated with water. Yakṣa's energy projected forth gods says the above quoted hymn. We know that according to the cosmogonical myths Prajāpati (Brahmā) first appeared on the cosmic waters[70]. These two – metaphysics and myth – overlapped each other in the Puranic period, the result of which can be seen in a beautiful sculpture from Deogarh, Jhansi (U.P.), belonging to the Gupta period (Plate 8). Lord Viṣṇu (Yakṣa of *Atharva–Veda*) is reclining on the back of cosmic waters, symbolised by the serpent king Śeśanāga. The gods around Lord Viṣṇu are Brahmā on the lotus. On Brahmā's right is Indra atop his mount elephant Airavat. On the extreme left is Kārtikeya on a peacock. On Brahmā's left are Śiva and Pārvatī astride on the bull Nandi.

---

68 *tama āsīt tamasā guḷham agre*
apraketaṁ salilaṁ sarvam ā idam /
tucchyenābhu apihitaṁ yad āsīt
tapasas tan mahinājāyataikam // RV 10. 129.3

The verse has been translated with the help of the translations by Geldner (Ṛgveda, Pt. III, p. 360) and Macdonell (*Vedic Reader*, p. 209)

69 *mahad yakṣaṁ bhuvanasya madhye*
tapasi krāntaṁ salilasya pṛṣṭhe /
tasmin śrāyante ya u ke ca devā
vṛkṣasya skandaḥ paritaḥ iva śākhā // AV 10.7.38

70 See p. 23.

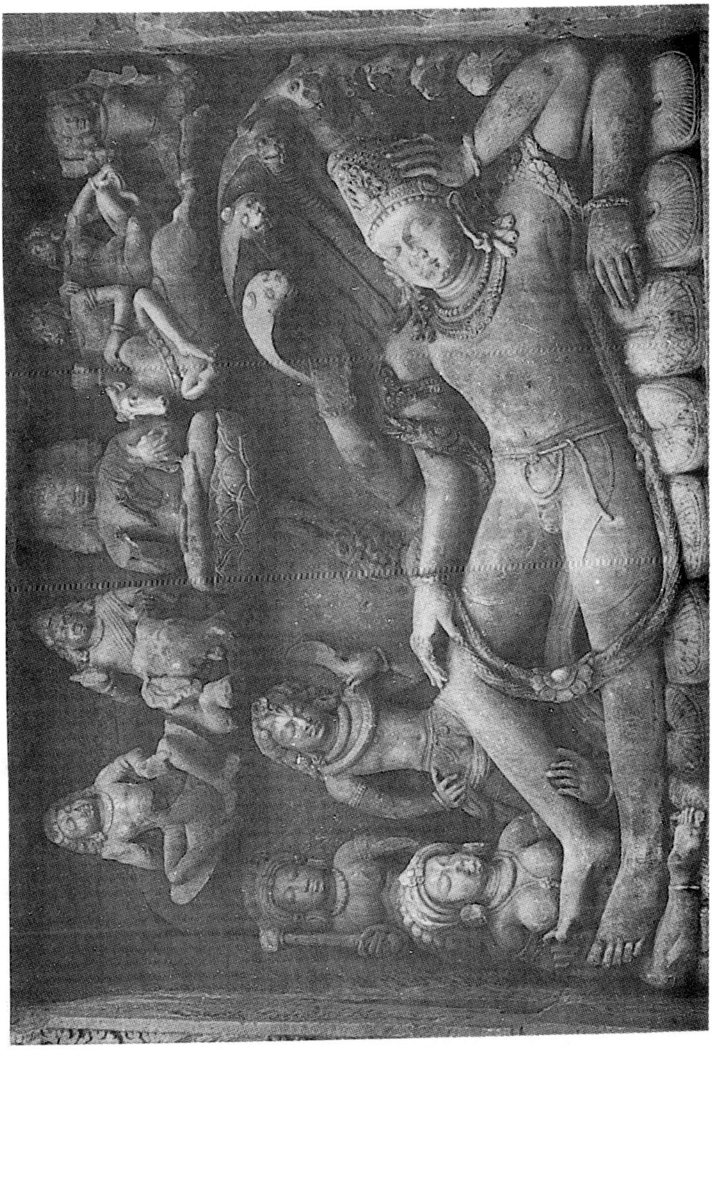

Plate 8: Viṣṇu, Reclining on Śeśanāga, 6th C. AD., Deogarh

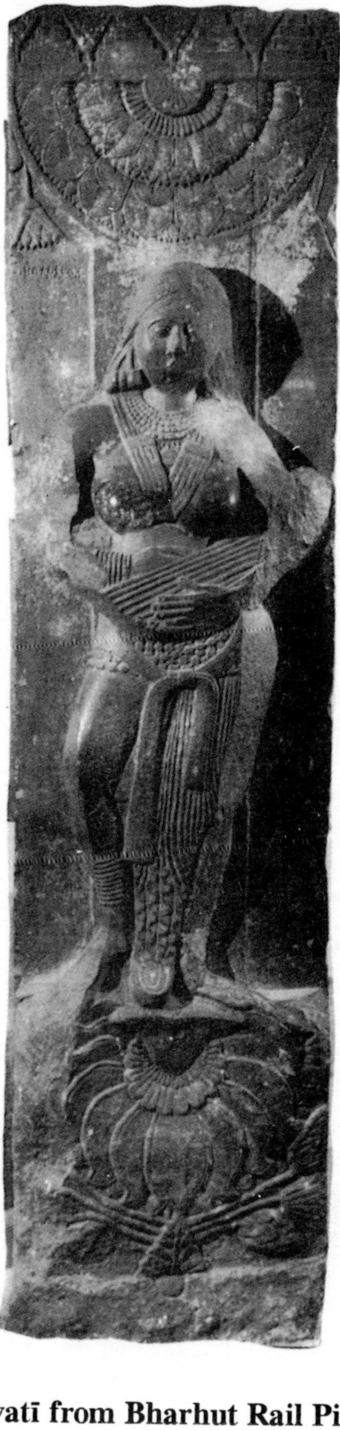

Plate 9: Sarasvatī from Bharhut Rail Pillar, 2nd C. BC.

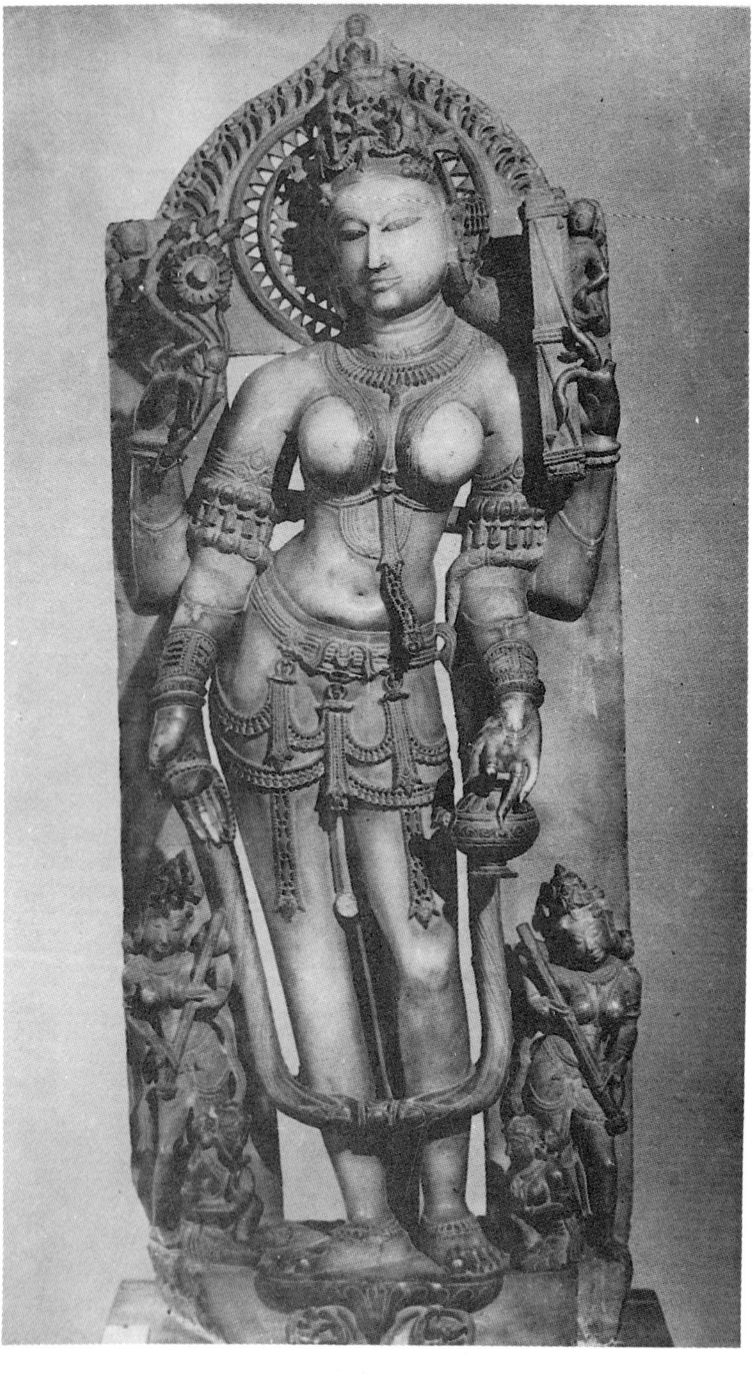

Plate 10: Sarasvatī 12th C. AD. Bikaner, Rajasthan

2.10 SARASVATĪ

Let us revert back to the passage from the *Maitrāyaṇī Saṁhita* (4.3.9), where it is said that one third of Varuṇa's virility entered Sarasvatī, 'which is water'[71]. Sarasvatī in her turn has been identified with *vāk* (speech, language) in many Vedic passages – *vāk vai sarasvatī*[72]. In one of the laudatory verses of a later period in praise of the *gāyatrī-mantra* it is said, *sarasvatī yā sāvitrī tvām vande vedamātaram*'[73]. The epithet *sarasvatī* for *gāyatrī*, the mother of knowledge (*vedamātaram*) is very significant. Sarasvatī was the principal river in the Vedic age. Its banks were dotted with *tapovanas* or hermitages, which were centres for learning. Many of the hymns were first uttered in those hermitages. Surely *gāyatrī-mantra*, which was considered as the best among the sacred hymns (*gāyatrı chandasāmaham* – *Gītā* 10.35), most probably owes its origin at the bank of the river Sarasvatī. It can be said that Sarasvatī inspired the seers who resided in these hermitages, to compose the hymns. She is identified with knowledge (*veda*) and speech (*vāk*), which enabled the seers to express their knowledge in the forms of hymns. The seers of the Vedic age were thankful to the power of speech - a privilege of human beings. Consequently power of speech or *vāk* was considered divine. In the *Taittirīya Brāhmaṇa* a worshipper prays to the deified *vāk*: 'Her, the Divine Speech, with offering we pray'.[74] Not only *vāk* is deified Sarasvatī, the river, she is also one of the Vedic goddesses in whose praise there are two whole hymns in the *Ṛg-Veda*. In these she is called 'the best of rivers, the best of goddesses, the best of mothers' (*nadītame devītame ambitame sarasvatī*).

The two aspects of Sarasvatī – the river and speech, both celebrated as goddesses, inseparable in the Vedic age were separated in a later period and Sarasvatī, the goddess of Speech (*vākdevī*) was imagined as standing or sitting on a lotus (Plates 9 and 10). In

---

71 See supra p. 45. *Sarasvatī* is derived from *saras* = anything flowing, large sheet of water etc. (Cf. Monier- Williams, Sanskrit English Dictionary)

72 SB 2.5.4.6; 3.1.4.9,14 and in other passages also.

73 *Sāvitrī* is the Sun and *gāyatrī* is the light, the resplendence, the lustre behind the sun. *Gāyatrī* is the benevolent mother of the universe.

74 *tām devīṁ vācam haviṣā yajāmahe.* TB 2.8.8.

association with Sarasvatī lotus, the symbol of water is reminiscent of her Vedic character[75].

2.11 Śrī – Lakṣmī

The lotus is the embodied essence of water, as has been asserted in the myths. In the *Gītā,* Śrī Kṛṣṇa, while explaining his omnipresence in all the things that exist in this world, says: 'I being *soma,* whose essence is *rasa* nourish all plants'.[76] Lotus being the embodiment of this *rasa* is a symbol of fertility in connection with the goddess Śrī-Lakṣmī. She has been invoked in one of the later additions to the *Ṛg-Veda* called the *Khilya*-hymns[77]. She is the older conception of Lakṣmī, the goddess of wealth and is inseparably associated with lotus, some of her names being *padmālayā* (one who dwells in the lotus), *padma* (from *padmā* – lotus) etc. In the hymns to Śrī (*Śrī-Sūkta*) it is said that she drives out wretchedness and non-prosperity[78]. In other words she brings prosperity. 'Mud' and 'Moisture'[79] are her two sons. Throughout the hymns the goddess is entreated to bestow prosperity. In ancient India the conception of prosperity consisted mainly of cattle and crop. As dispenser of crop she enjoys descriptive names of *ārdrā* (moist), *puṣkariṇī* and *padminimī* (both mean ponds full of lotuses). Earth and water are the two chief ingredients, whose combination produces fertility. In connection with Śrī-Lakṣmī lotus, being a representative of earth and water (out of the combination of

---

75 Sarasvatī, the Hindu goddess of wisdom and knowledge has her counterpart in Mahayana Buddhism in the conception of the deity Prajñāpāramitā. She is the personification of wisdom (*prajñā*), the highest virtue *(pāramitā*), which leads to nirvana. Goddess Sarasvatī is the wife of the creator Brahmā. Prajñāpāramitā is the female aspect of the universal Buddha (Ādibuddha). Like Brahmā Ādibuddha is also self-born.

76 *puṣṇāmi ca ausadhīḥ sarvāḥ somo bhutvā rasātmakaḥ* Gītā 15.13

77 Cf. J. Scheftelowitz, Die Apokryphen des Ṛgveda, and 'Śrī-Sūkta' in ZDMG, 75 (1921), pp.37ff.

78 *kṣutpipāsāmalāṁ jyeṣṭhām alakṣmīṁ nāśayāmy aham/*
abhūtim asamṛddhiṁ ca sarvaṁ nirṇuda me gṛhāt // Sri-Sukta 8

79 *kardama* and *ciklita*, see verses 11,12.

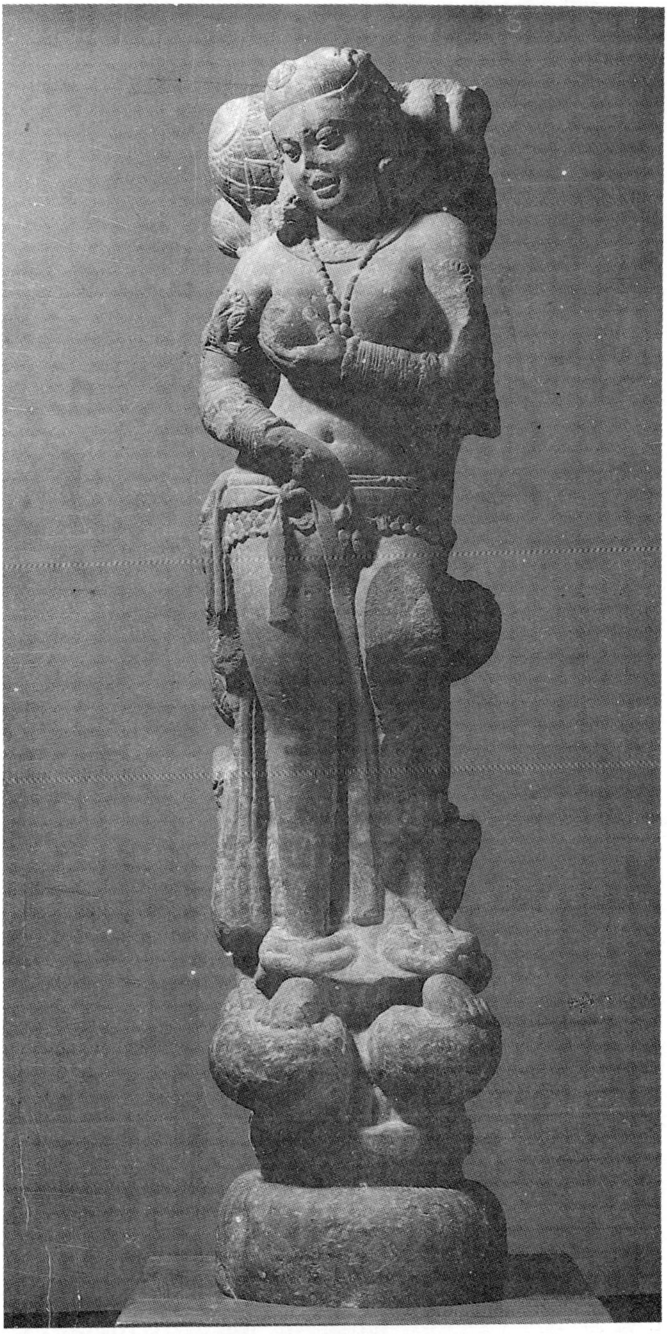

Plate 11 A: Śrī Lakṣmī, Kushana statuette (front), from Mathurā, 1st C. AD.

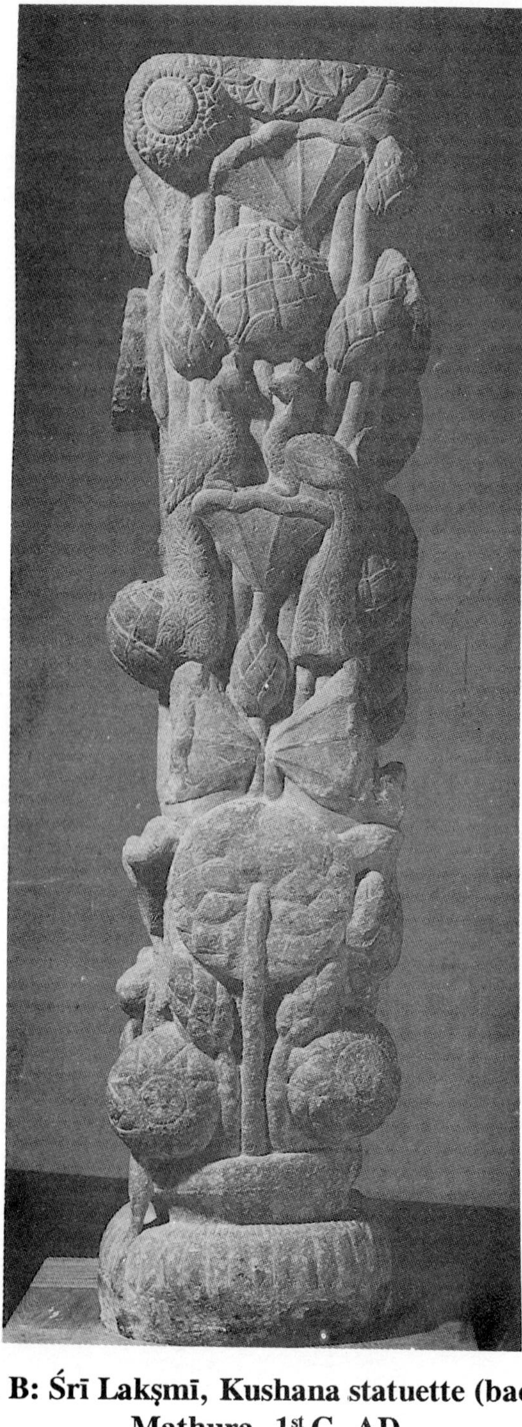

Plate 11 B: Śrī Lakṣmī, Kushana statuette (back), from Mathura, 1st C. AD.

these two elements the lotus springs forth) and the embodied essence of nourishment symbolises fertility on which prosperity and wealth depended in those times[80].

The Kushana statuette of Śrī-Lakṣmī (Plate 11) is the earliest representation of the goddess on stone. This sculpture is virtually the hymns of *Śrī-Sūkta* transferred on to stone. It is an interpretation of the hymns by an unknown artist. Goddess Śrī is standing on two lotuses coming out of a brimming vessel (*pūrṇa-ghaṭam*). With her left hand she is holding her right breast. This posture means she nourishes the living beings. Lotuses are gushing forth from the brimming vessel, the symbol of never ending spring of life and she is surrounded with these flowers. It indicates abundance and prosperity. This piece of art is a visual presentation of verse 8 of *Śrī-Sūkta* in which she has been requested to bar poverty and wretchedness. Standing amidst a profusion of lotus plants, she is prosperity and abundance personified.

Adjectives like 'gold hued' (*suvarṇā*), 'sitting on a lotus', 'lotus-hued', (*padme sthitā padma-varṇā – Śrī-Sūkta*, verse 4) present a picture of a beautiful goddess. Hence later on the word *śrī* came to denote beauty, though primarily the word meant prosperity and fortune. H. Oldenberg thinks the primary meaning of *śrī* in the Ṛgvedic times was *Schönheit* (beauty)[81]. J.Gonda and Gerda Hartmann say *śrī* does not primarily mean 'beauty' but 'fertility, abundance, fortune'.[82] In modern Bengali usage this word has retained both the meanings – prosperity as well as beauty[83]. *Śrī* meaning abundance, prosperity is to be found in the first fifteen verses, which are supposed to be older than the rest[84]. In the rest of the verses, which belong to

---

80 Coomaraswamy says,' ...fundamentally, the goddess of the lotus (i.e. Sri-Laksmi – author) is a figure of Abundance' in Origin of the Buddha Image, p. 35.

81 Cf NGGW, Part 1, Berlin 1918, p.44.

82 J. Gonda, *Aspects of Early Visnuism*, Utrecht 1954, p.211 and G. Hartmann, Beiträge zur Geschichte der Göttin Laksmi, Thesis, p.7

83 '*shri vriddhi'* means getting prosperous. But when *'shri'* is used for describing the features of a girl as in *meyetir shri ache'* then the word points to the comely beauty of a girl.

84 J.Scheftelowitz, *Apokryphen des Rgveda*, p. 75, and Śrī-Sūkta, op. cit., p. 41.

a later period, the beauty of Śrī-Lakṣmī has been described and this word also comes to mean 'beauty'. In these verses her face, thighs and eyes have been compared to a lotus (*padmānane padma-uru padmākṣi padma-sambhave* – verse 17). She also wears a lotus garland around her neck (*padma-mālinī)*. Although the association of the lotus and goddess Śrī-Lakṣmī has a special significance the comparison of her face, thighs and the eyes to lotus as a standard of judgement of beauty, starts from this period. In the Canonical Pāli literature one comes often across such similes, whenever an example of soft glowing beauty of a person is described. The beautiful face of Subhā, a Buddhist nun (*therī*) has been compared to a lotus bud: "in your beautiful gleaming face, which is to be compared to a lotus..."[85] Eyes (*Thera Apadāna* 528.2, 535.13), feet (*Jātaka* 151, 547; *Therī Apadana* 17.39) and skin (*padumottarattacā* – skin more beautiful than the lotus) have also been compared to the lotus.

In the pillar medallion from Bharhut (Plate 12) goddess Laksmi is flanked by two elephants. All the three figures are either sitting or standing on lotuses, the symbol of fertility in connection with Śrī (or Lakṣmī of later period). The elephants (*gaja*) are pouring water on the deity of prosperity and who also nourishes all the living beings, visually presented by her posture of holding her left breast with her right hand as in the Kushana statuette (Pl. 11).

Elephants have a special significance in relation to the goddess Lakṣmī. They are considered as forms of clouds on earth. With their magical power they charm the clouds to bless the earth with abundant rain.[86] Abundant rain helps the earth

---

85 *uppalasikharopamānite vimale hāṭakasannibha mukhe. Therīgāthā* 382.
86 Cf. H. Zimmer, Mythen und Symbole, p.117-122 The king of gods, Indra's mount is the elephant *airāvat* (son of *iravat*). *Irā* means fluid and *irāvat* is cloud. *Irāvatī* is the ancient name of Ravi, one of the five rivers of Punjab. According to Vedic mythology Indra releases water from clouds and hence *airāvat*, son of *irāvat* (cloud) is an appropriate name of his mount.

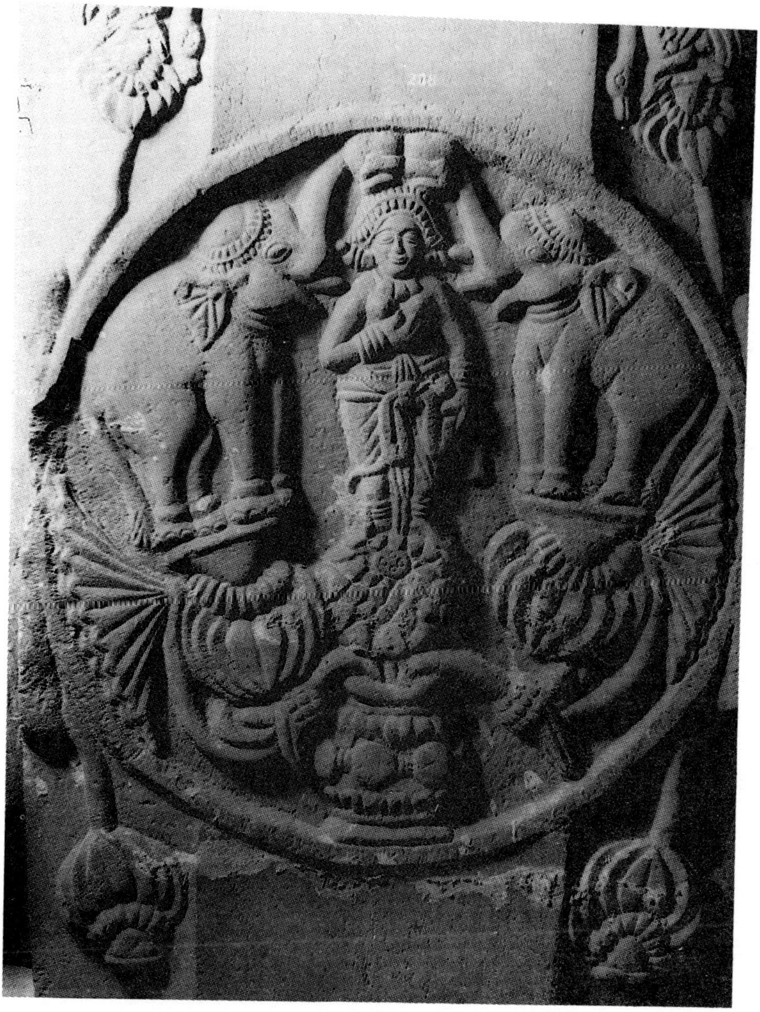

Plate 12: Gaja-Lakṣmī from Bharhut pillar Medallion, 2 C. BC.

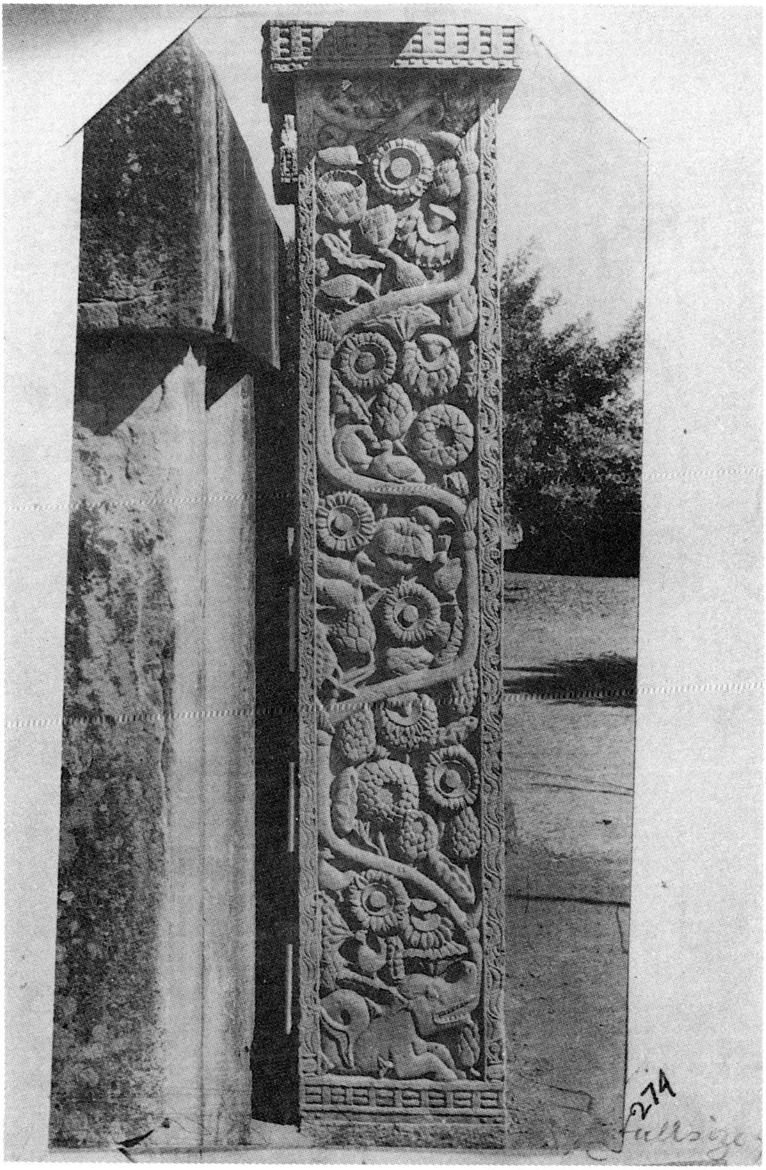

Plate 13: Sanchi, west gate south face of the right pillar, CA. 1st C. BC.

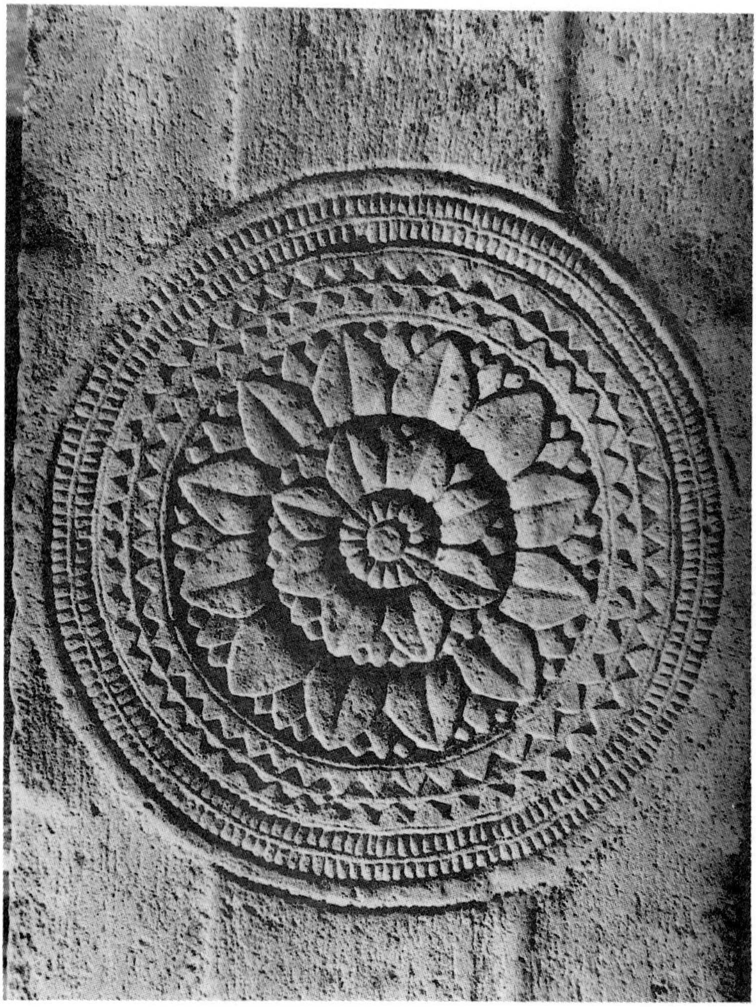

Plate 14: Medallion, Sanchi stupa 2, ca. 1st C. BC.

to produce abundant crop, which brings prosperity and prosperity is the domain of goddess Lakṣmī or Śrī of the Khilya hymns of the *Ṛg-Veda*.

The epithet *padmamālinī* of Śrī-Lakṣmī shows that lotus garland was worn as an ornament. Though this accessory of personal adornment was in vogue from the early Vedic times (e.g. *puṣkarasraja*) it was worn more as a symbol of power than as an embellishment by gods and men, who wanted to gain power (see p.44). The lotus garland only as an ornament, shorn of symbolic meanings started to gain popularity from the later Vedic period, to which *Śrī-Sūkta* belong and continued its sway during the Buddhist period. The lotus flower was one of the most beloved ornaments during the time of the Buddha. King Mahāsudarśana planted lotuses in tanks so that everyone in his kingdom could have lotuses all the year round for making ornaments (*Dīghanikāya* 17.1.23).[87] The lotus as a decorative element not only heightened the beauty of human beings but also of the surroundings. King Suddhodana, the father of Prince Siddhārtha, laid out lotus ponds for the beautification of the surroundings of the Prince.[88] These were meant for aesthetic pleasure and enjoyment (*pokkharaṇī nāma yattha katthaci manussānāṁ kīlituṁ ramituṁ katā hoti*).[89]

The profusion of lotus in the Buddhist plastic art reflects the preference of the Buddhist texts towards these flowers, as is evident from the carved lotuses on the pillars and gates of Sanchi and Bharhut stupas[90] (Plates 13,14). Although in both the Vedic and Buddhist ages the lotus was considered as a beauty aid but there was a difference of approach towards this flower in these two ages. The Vedic seers of course appreciated

---

87 Cf. also *Mahasudarsana-Sutra (Jataka)* 1.57 – 60.

88 *mama sudaṁ bhikkhave pitu nivasane pokkharanīyo kāritā honti, ekattha sudaṁ uppalaṁ ekattha padumaṁ ekattha puṇḍarikaṁ yāvadeva mama atthāya.* AN 3.38.1.

89 *Vinaya Pitaka,*Vol. 4, *Bhikkhuni Vibhanga, Pacittiya* 41.

90 FDK Bosch opines that in the Buddhist sculpture in Bharhut and Sanchi the "faculty of bestowing life, fertility and wealth is attributed to the lotus plant and its vital points" – The Golden Germ, p. 49.

its beauty, but hardly mentioned it in such unequivocal language. Only once in the *Ṛg-Veda* a poet alludes to the beauty of a lotus pond in a verse: 'This house of hospitality is like a lotus pond. It is decorated like a wonderful palace of Gods'.[91]

2.12 Righteousness

From the previous discussions we know that a close relation between divinity and lotus-pond existed in the mind of the Vedic people. In the *Athrva-Veda* it is said, one who offers *viṣṭārin* enters heaven and finds a place in the lotus pond.[92] Lotus ponds were held in such high esteem that its beauty was compared to the dwelling of gods[93] and were regarded as divine manifestations. While recounting various misfortunes and catastrophes, which are likely to befall a kingdom, where law or truth is transgressed, a poet says:

> 'Not in his field a lotus-pond, the bulb-bearing lotus or lotus-stalk comes into existence, in whose kingdom a Brahmaṇa's wife is obstructed even through ignorance.'[94]

This verse reflects the Vedic concept of the ideal kingship, under whose hegemony the country is supposed to prosper. In those times prosperity depended on the fertility of soil, as agriculture was the main source of wealth. Fertility, in turn, depended on timely rainfall. 'Rain means crop' (*annam khalu vai varṣam* – TS 5.4.9.2) was the maxim of the time and folk-belief made rainfall dependent on justice. In the *Śatapatha Brāhmaṇa* it is expressly said:

> The water is the law. Hence whenever the water comes down to this world, everything here comes

---

91 *bhojasyedaṁ puṣkariṇīva veṣma / pariṣkṛtam devamāneva citram //* RV 10.107.10

92 See p. 39.

93 See Footnote 91.

94 *nāsya kṣetre puṣkariṇī nāṇḍikam jāyate bisam /*
yasmin rāṣṭre nirudhyate brahmajāyācityā // AV 5.17.16

to be in accordance with the law. But whenever there is drought, then the stronger seizes upon the weaker, for the water is the law.[95]

The Vedic people believed that transgression of law or moral order resulted in drought. To counter that catastrophe Varuṇa, the guardian of *ṛta* (i.e. cosmic order, laws of nature, moral order rolled into one) is often besought to send rain.[96] The view that drought and transgression of law were interdependent was prevalent also in the post-Vedic period. Affliction of drought was attributed to the transgression of law. The story of the one-horned sage Ṛṣyaśṛṅga, born of a doe, is told in the *Vanaparva* of the epic *Mahābhārata*.[97] King Lomapāda had been guilty of falsehood towards a *brāhmaṇa*, which caused drought in his kingdom. Sage Ṛṣyaśṛṅga was called and he rescued the kingdom from the clutches of drought by his piety. In ancient India law, truth and justice were practically synonymous. People believed in the interdependence of rain and truth (= law, justice): 'Water is indeed truth. Therefore, it is said, that it is a manifestation of truth as the water flows.'[98] When a king oppresses a *brāhmaṇa*'s wife (tantamount to transgression of law) then there are no rain, no ponds and consequently no lotus. Here lack of lotus-ponds means lack of divine blessings. It may be noted that the Indian peasantry still believes drought is the divine retribution against sinful acts.

95 *dharmo vā āpas tasmād yademaṁ lokam āpo āgacchanti sarvam evedaṁ yathā dharmaṁ bhavaty atha yadā vṛṣṭir bhavati baliyam eva tarhy abaliyam ādatte dharmo hi āpaḥ*. SB 11.1.6.24

96 See p. 33.

97 Chapters 110 – 113.

98 *āpo hi vai satyaṁ tasmā yenapo yānti tat satyasya rūpam ity āhuḥ*. SB 7.4.1.6.

3

Symbol of Non-Attachment

The example of the capability of the flowers and leaves of lotus plant to remain unsullied by mud and water is a much-discussed phenomenon in the Buddhist literature. The Vedic sages do not mention this unique characteristic either in the four Vedas or in the numerous books that followed the Vedas, viz. the *Brāhmaṇas* and *Āraṅyakas*. Only in the last phase of the Vedic literature, i.e. in the *Upaniṣads* this feature is mentioned, but that also sparingly. In the *Chandogya Upanisad* the example of the relation of a lotus leaf and water elucidates the mental condition of one who knows Brahman (*bramajñānī*) in this world: 'As water does not cling to the lotus leaf, so evil does not cling to one who knows it.'[99] In the *Maitrāyaṇī Upaniṣad* the comparison has been put in the other way. The undying soul is the drop of water on the lotus, i.e. the body.[100]

From the scanty references to the lotus or its leaf as a symbol of non-attachment it is obvious, that in the Vedic period it was not a popular way of expression. By the time of the Buddha this example from nature had gained popularity and the Pāli Canons teem with references to this particular characteristic of this plant. It became a standard example to illustrate the mental condition of a spiritual person. In the Buddhist text rules of discipline have been laid down for

---

99 *yathā puṣkarapalāśa āpo na śliṣyante evam evamvidhi pāpaṁ karmam na śliṣyanta iti*. Ch. U. 4.14.3; cf. also Gītā 5.10: *lipyate na sa pāpena padmapatram iva ambhasā.*

100 *atha ya ha khalu vā va śarīra ityuktaṁ sa bhūtātmetyuktam athāmṛto 'syātmā binduriva puṣkara iti.* Mai. Up. 3.2.

acquiring supreme knowledge and thereby attain nirvāna. One can thus make oneself free from the shackles and cycles of birth and rebirth. The practice of mental training is one such step towards the highest goal, which includes guarding the doors of sensual world:

> So the something agreeable or disagreeable or neutral is stilled and poised indifference is established. Just as on an upstanding lotus leaf, as yet unfurled, drops of water come about it but finding no resting place glide off, so, O Ānanada, with the same speed, swiftness and ease indifference (*upekkhā*) is established and something agreeable or disagreeable or which is both agreeable and disagreeable is laid to rest. This is called o Ānanda, consummate development of faculties in the Rule of Noble with references to the odours the nose smells.[101]

Various stages of spiritual progress have been compared to the different stages of the lotus till it blossoms and to the plants relation to water to make these stages comprehensible to the laity:

> Even as in the pond of blue lotuses or in a pond of red lotuses or in a pond of white lotuses, a few red, blue or white lotuses are born in the water, grow in the water, do not rise above the water but thrive while altogether immersed. A few, blue, red or white lotuses are born in the water and reach the surface of the water. A few blue, red or white lotuses are born in the water, grow in the water and stand up rising out of the water, undefiled by

---

101 *tassa taṁ uppanaṁ manāpaṁ uppanaṁ amanāpaṁ uppannaṁ manāpāmanāpaṁ nirujjhati, upekhā saṇṭhāti, seyyathāpi ānanda īsakopaṇe paduminipatte udakaphusitāni pavattanti na saṇṭhānti, evaṁ eva kho ānanda, yassa kassaci evaṁ sīghaṁ evam tuvaṭaṁ evaṁ appakasirena uppannaṁ manāpaṁ uppannaṁ amanāpaṁ uppannaṁ manāpāmanāpaṁ nirujjhati upekhā saṇṭhāti, ayaṁ vuccata. ānanda, ariyassa vinaye anuttarā indriya-bhāvanā ghāna-viññeyyesu gandhesu. Majjhimanikaya* 132 (III.300).

> water. Even so, did the Lord, surveying the world with the eye of an awakened one, see beings with little dust in their eyes, with acute faculties, with dull faculties, of good disposition, of bad disposition, docile, indocile few seeing fear in sins and the world beyond.'[102]

The negative relation of lotus to water is the prevalent thought in the Buddhist texts as far as the lotus is concerned. But there is also reference to their positive relation to illustrate one of the stages of mental condition. In that stage one engaged in meditation drenches his body with 'satisfaction without zest' (Pāli: *nippitikena sukhena*), just as a lotus is drenched from root to tip by cool waters[103]. Before the meditator reaches the final goal he has to pass through various stages of spiritual experiences. In one of the penultimate stages 'I am' (*asmīti*) conceit still lurks in the mind of the meditator, which he has to overcome. Venerable Khemeka says, 'a meditator, before he becomes an *arhat* (worthy, venerable), in whom all the *āsavas* (influences) are destroyed, is in that stage where he realises 'I am' in the Five-Grasping-Groups (*pañca-upādāna-khandha*). According to the Buddhist philosophy the empirical personality, which consists of only five groups (*khandha*), is the storage point of all the sufferings. The five groups are: (i) *rūpa* (body) with its six sense organs – eyes, ears, nose, tongue, organs of touch and of thinking (*manas*); (ii) *vedanā* (sensation, feeling) i.e. sense-impressions, which lead to (iii) *saññā* (perception). This again reflects the objects in mind of the observer. From such perceptions (iv) *saṅkhāra* (mental agitations) are born, viz., notions, longings, lusts, and motives for deeds. At the end (v) *viññāna* (awareness) arises from perception[104]. In this five-groups the meditator is exhausted and what remains is 'Not-I' (*anattā; attā = ātman*).[105] After this realisation he

102 These lines from *Mahavagga* of *Vinaya Pitaka* (1.5.11-12) are often repeated in the other canonical Pali texts also: DN 14.3.6; MN 26 (1.169); SN 6.1.6.12; Mn 359, 453 etc.

103 *Dīghanikāya* 2.80

104 See H.W. Schumann, Der historische Buddha, pp. 156-157.

105 *Ibid*, p. 84.

advances towards the final stage. To make the conception of *pañca-upādāna-khandha* intelligible to his followers, Venerable Khemaka gives the example of a lotus flower, whose scent belongs to no individual part but to the whole flower:

> Just as, Brothers, in the case of the scent of a blue lotus or white lotus or red lotus, if one should say, 'the scent belongs to the petals or the colours or the fibres of it' would he be rightly be describing the scent?[106]

'Lotuses are born in the water, grow in the water and stand up rising out of the water, undefiled by water' epitomises the mental condition of the Lord on whom the sensual world had no influence. The Buddha uses this simile to illustrate his position in this world:

> 'Just as, o Monks, a blue, red or white lotus, though born in water grows up in water when it reaches the surface stands there unsoiled by water, just so, o Brahmin, though born in the world, grown up in the world, having overcome the world, I abide unsoiled by the world. Take it, that I am a Buddha, Brahmin'[107]

In the *Jātaka* there are several tales about Bodhisattva's non-attachment to the world symbolised by a lotus. The *Jātaka* stories are the tales about previous births of Lord Buddha, where he is called Bodhisattva, which means, in whom the essential qualities of a future Buddha exist but he takes birth in

---

106 *seyyathāpi, āvuso, uppalassa vā padumassa vā puṇḍarīkassa vā gandho. yo nu kho evaṁ vadeyya pattassa gandho ti vaṇṇassa gandho ti kiñjakkhasso gandho ti vā sammā nu kho vadamāno vadeyyāti.* SN 22.89.21

107 *seyyathāpi bhikkhave uppalaṁ vā padumaṁ vā puṇḍarīkaṁ vā udake jātaṁ udake saṁvaḍḍhaṁ udakāṁ accugamma thāti anupalittaṁ udakena, evaṁ eva kho brāhmaṇa loke jāto loke saṁvaḍḍho lokaṁ abhibhuyya viharāmi anupalitto lokena buddho ti māṁ brāhmaṇa dhārehīti.* AN 4.36.3.

Cf. *yathāpi udake jātaṁ puṇḍarīkaṁ pavaḍḍhati*
na upalippati toyena sucigandhaṁ manoramaṁ /
tathā eva loke sujāto buddho lokevirajjati
na upalippati lokena toyena padumaṁ yathā // Aṅguttara Nikāya 6.43.2.

order to help mankind to attain nirvāna. *Khadiraṅgāra Jātaka* is one such story. It narrates the story of Bodhisattva who was barred by Māra, the Satan of Buddhist mythology, from giving alms to a *paccekabuddha* (one, who is enlightened but does not share his knowledge with others). Māra created a pit of red, hot embers before Bodhisattva's dwelling. Bodhisattva, undaunted by this, strode right into the pit of fire. All of a sudden a big lotus sprang up to support his feet. The appearance of lotus under the feet of Buddha or Bodhisattva is an oft-mentioned phenomenon in the Buddhist texts. *Lalitavistara*, a book of the Mahāyana Buddhism, reports that after his birth as soon as the Bodhisattva stepped on the earth, the earth opened up and from that pit a big lotus sprang up. Standing on that lotus Bodhisattva looked in all the directions. Lotuses also sprang up wherever Bodhisattva kept his feet.[108] In these stories lotuses underneath Bodhisattva's feet symbolises Bodhisattva's indifference towards the world.

A very peculiar botanical characteristic of the lotus is that though it is a water-born flower, it remains undefiled by it. The water does not cling to its leaves and petals but glides away. Māra, the evil one, symbolises a worldly phenomenon while Bodhisattva is divine and beyond this. As a footstool of Bodhisattva the lotus, which came out of the pit, signifies that as a human being Bodhisattva belonged to this world but he was above it and remained undefiled by it. Sin and impurity glided off him.

In the Buddhist literature lotus comes essentially as a symbol of non-attachment to the sensual world and the Buddha has been compared to it, which points to this characteristic of the flower. The ancient sculptors keeping in mind this simile considered an open lotus as the most appropriate seat for the Lord and carved accordingly. Once again that was the interpretation of the texts by the iconographers. The lotus as the seat of the Buddha presupposes the long tradition of Indian thinking where the lotus was always considered as seats of divine

108 S. Morenz and J. Schubert, Der Gott auf der Blume, p. 134.

beings. To this a natural characteristic of the flower that though born in the muddy water it rises above it and remains unsullied was added during the Buddhist period. Lotus seat for the Buddha became a symbol of nirvana.

In the sculpture from Sarnath the Buddha is sitting on an open lotus (Plate 15). In the ancient books of iconography (*śilpaśāstra*) various kinds of seats are mentioned. One of these is *padmāsana*, which is an open lotus in circular or oval shape used as a seat or pedestal (*pīṭha*).[109] The sitting posture of the Lord is also called *padmāsana*. In this posture legs are kept crossed and the feet rest upon the thighs with upturned soles.[110] His hand gesture (*mudrā*) signifies *dharma-cakra-pravartana,* i.e. his first discourse at Sarnath setting the wheel of *dharma* (religion) in motion.

In Buddhist iconography a lotus flower atop a pillar is a common sight. A lotus flower with hanging petals and raised torus on top of a pillar, which serves as base for an animal sculpted on it are known as the lotus-capitals, although some critics prefer to call these bell-capitals. James Fergusson[111] and Sir John Marshall[112] opine that these Mauryan pillars with metal like polish and finish have a Persepolitan origin and it is not lotus which is on the top of the pillar but an inverted bell, which was also copied from its Persopolitan prototype by the Indian sculptors. A.K. Mitra is of the opinion that "the Muryan type of bell-capital with its characteristic petals and an animal sculpture above implies a fusion of Achaemenid and Hellenistic element."[113] Craven says, the abacus is a "fluted bell"[114] and in Goetz's opinion these capitals are "elegant bells made of lotus petals".[115] But art historians like E.B. Havell and A.K. Coomaraswamy refute a foreign origin of these capitals. Havell

109 T.A.G. Rao, *Elements of Hindu Iconography*, Description of Terms, p. 19.
110 *Ibid*, p. 18.
111 *Indian and Eastern Art*, Vol. 1, p.59
112 *Cambridge History of India*, Vol. 1, pp.621 - 622.
113 "A Bell-Capital from Bhuvaneshwar " in *IHQ*, Vol. V, p.698.
114 Roy C. Craven, *Indian Art*, p. 40.
115 H. Goetz, Indien, p. 47: "eine elegante 'Glocke' aus Lotosblättern."

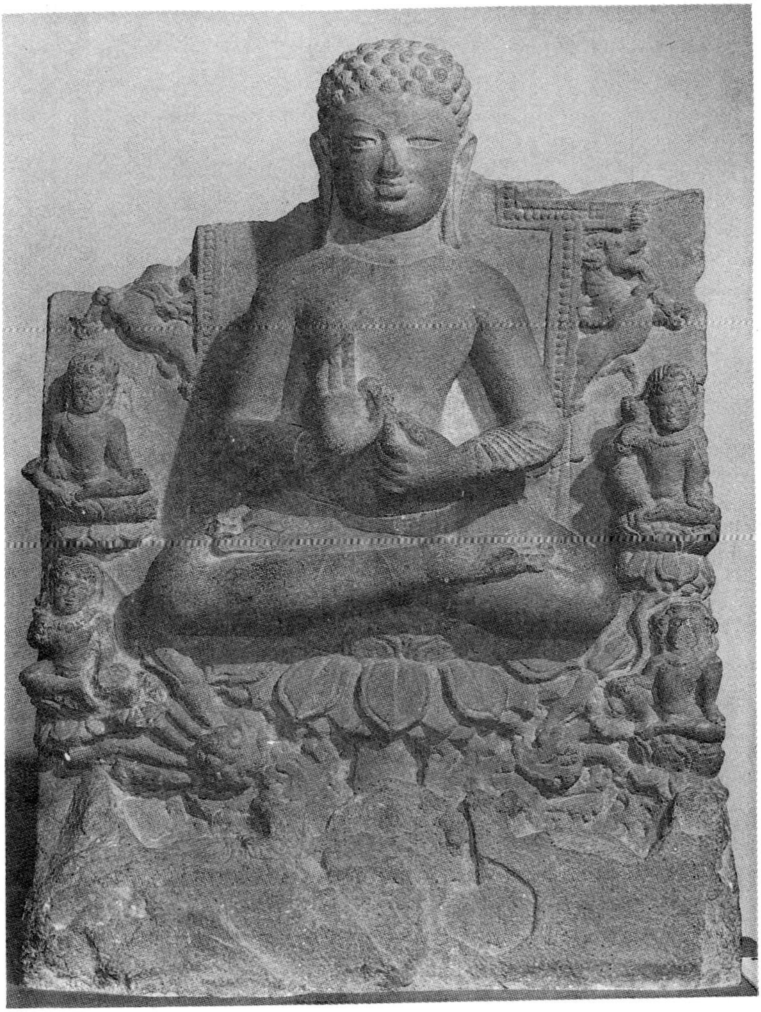

Plate 15: The Buddha, Sarnath, Gupta period, CA. 6th C. AD

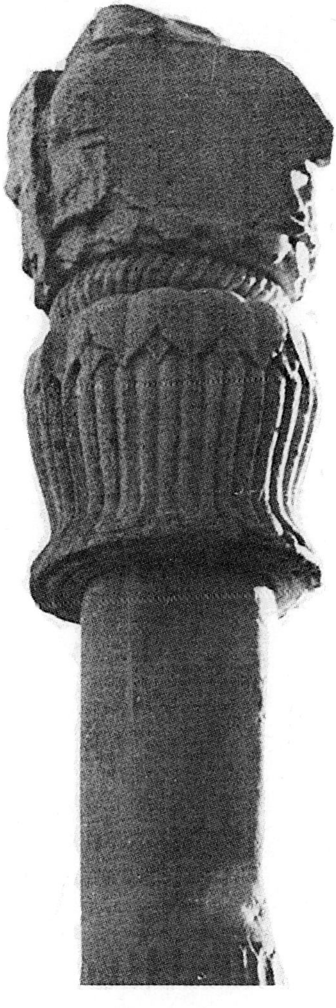

Plate 16: Lotus-capital, Besnagar Pillar, ca. 140 BC

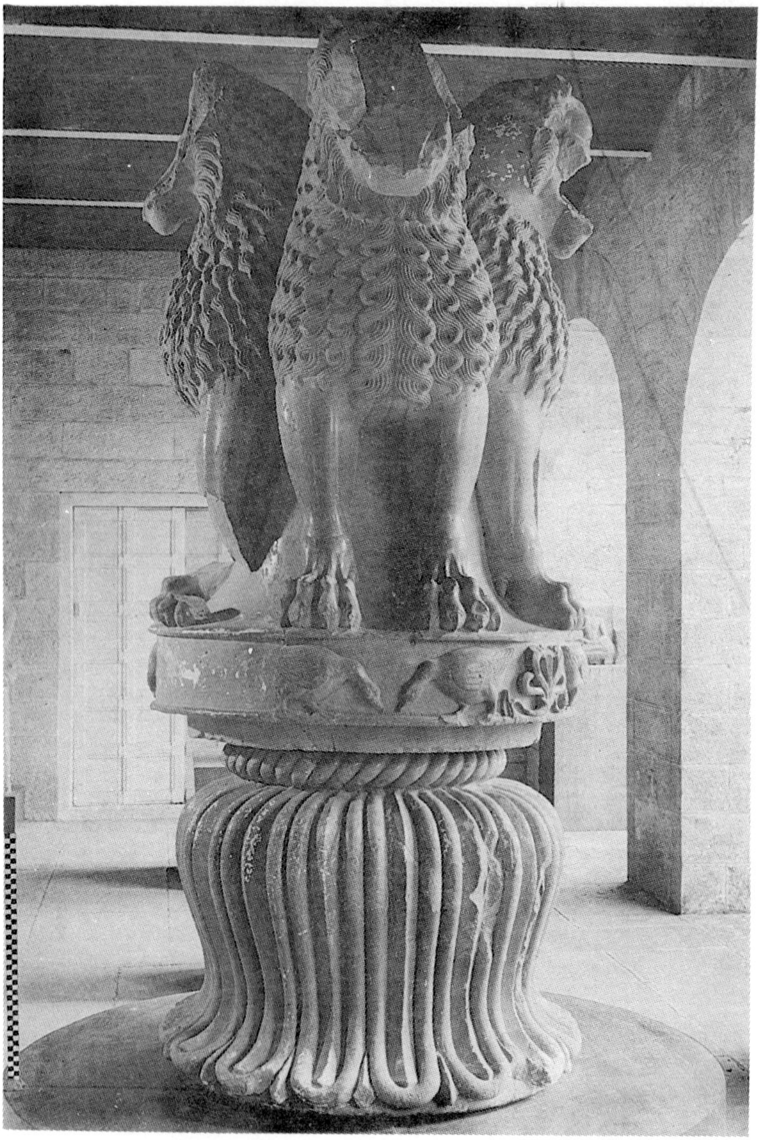

Plate 17: Lotus-capital (Also known as Lion-Capital) Sanchi, CA. 150 BC

says, "Moreover, the Bharhut and Sanchi sculptures show us that symbolism of Asoka's pillars has nothing to do with a bell, but is an adaptation to structural purposes of the same lotus-and-vase motive, which with a different implication, served for a symbol of the Buddha's nativity."[116] According to Coomaraswamy, "Early literary sources will be found to yield a satisfactory explanation of the use of lotus as a support."[117]

We have observed that the lotus has traditionally been imagined as a support and in the sculpture lotus has been shown sometimes with raised torus with its petals hanging down. The petals of the lotus from Bharhut (Figure 6) have the same form and shape as those of the lotus atop other Buddhist pillars. Moreover, the lotus on the Besnagar pillar (Plate 16) has three rows of petals all hanging down, which makes it evident that the sculptor had a lotus in mind. Moreover, it was not uncommon to carve lotus with hanging petals as shown in the figures 6 and 7. On the face of such evidences it can be said that the lotus-capitals are indigenous in origin but probably executed, as Havell suggests, by "skilled Persian masons attracted to Asoka's court by the fame of the great emperor."[118] The lotus capitals are an essential part of Buddhist sculpture. Lotus on top of the pillars serves as a base for a lion or lions (Plates 16,17). The lion represents Śākyasiṁha – the lion (or king) of the Sākyas, i.e. Gautama Buddha and the four lions symbolise the preaching of the Lord in all the four directions.

---

116 E.B. Havell, *A Handbook of Indian Art*, p. 41.
117 "Origin of lotus-(so-called Bell) capitals" in *IHQ*, VI, 1930, pp. 373 ff.
118 E.B. Havell, ibid, p. 40. Craven and Goetz also support this theory.

4

DEVELOPMENT OF LOTUS CONCEPTION

The *Ṛg-Veda* is the earliest Indian document on religion, customs, institutions and society. Most of the hymns are laudatory verses in praise of the deities with the aim to propitiate them, although the metaphysical undertone of some of the hymns cannot be overlooked. These verses or a line from the verses were taken up like threads in the successive periods and were elaborated, philosophised and quoted in support of theses and propositions, propagated by the prevailing conceptions of the period. The *Atharva-Veda* was preoccupied with magic and popular beliefs, while the schools of the *Yajur-Veda*, *Brāhmaṇas* and *Āraṇyakas* with the liturgical side of the religion. Hence in the texts of this period metaphysics took the back seat. The Indian philosophy came to blossom in the age of *Upaniṣads*. During this period man's quest for eternity and freedom from the vicious circle of birth and rebirth are the main themes.

In the development of thoughts and conceptions regarding lotus in the Vedic literature three phases are noticeable. In the chronological order of the books as well as in the order of the development of thoughts references from the *Ṛg-Veda* and *Atharva-Veda* are the earliest ones. In both the books references to the lotus in connection with a deity or metaphysical conception serve as clues, pregnant with thought-provoking ideas. The expositions or explanations of these short but significant lines are not to be found in these two texts, as these two Vedas are written in verses. In this period the lotus has been mentioned in connection with (i) Agni, (ii) Heaven and Sun, (iii) Asvinā, (iv) Vasiṣṭha, (v) World-wheel, (vi) Womb, (vii) Immortality and (viii) Righteousness. (ix) Sarasvatī, the deified river is also mentioned but not in connection with the lotus, which is a later occurrence.

Most of the above ideas and conceptions were taken up in the second phase, to which the two schools of *Yajurveda* - Black and White - (*Taittirīya Saṁhitā, Maitrāyaṇī Saṁhitā* and *Vājasneyī Saṁhitā* belong to these schools), *Brāhmaṇas,* supplementary verses to the *Ṛg-Veda* (*Śrī-Sūkta* is a supplementary called *khilya* hymns) and *Āraṇyakas* belong. These texts lifted the lines as guiding thoughts, which were explained, furthered and in some ceases myths were woven round those conceptions to prove the truthfulness of the lines. Thus the Agni-verse of the *Ṛg-Veda* branches into: (i) Agni myth, (ii) Creation myth (cosmogony) or lotus and Prajāpati, (iii) relation of womb and lotus, (iv) lotus and Heaven/Sun, (v) explanation of *puṣkara-srajau* in reference to the Asvinā in the *Śatapatha Brāhmaṇa*, (vi) the *Śatapatha Brāhmaṇa's* exegesis of lotus ponds in the heaven and immortality, which is an exposition of the Atharvavedic verse and (vii) the identification of the river Sarasvatī with *vāk* (speech). In this process Sarasvatī comes to be associated with the lotus. Besides these, (viii) myths about the origin of lotus and (ix) Śrī-Lakṣmī and lotus are two new conceptions introduced during this period. The second phase, it can be said, is marked by exegeses, explanations and elaboration. The metaphysical problems in relation to lotus do not surface in this period. Another noticeable development is that the lotus serves as a simile (in *Śrī-Sūkta*), which was taken to its height in the classical period.

The third phase is dominated by metaphysics: (i) a verse from the *Atharva-Veda*, according to which lotus is the seat of Brahman[119], is the main theme as far as the *Upaniṣads* are

119 *puṇḍarīkaṁ navadvāraṁ tribhir guṇebhir āvṛtam /*
tasmin yat yakṣam ātamanvat tad vai brahmavido viduḥ // AV 10.8.43 (The lotus having nine doors is covered with three strands. What Yakṣa, which possesses soul, is in that (lotus), which the Brahman-knower knows.)
The lotus in connection with metaphysics comes in *Maitrayani Upaniṣad 6.2.; Kaivalya Upaniṣad* 6; *Mahānarāyaṇa Upaniṣad* 12.3; *Chāndogya Upaniṣad* 8.1.1.

concerned; (ii) the relation of water and lotus, that water does not cling to the lotus leaf, has been first expressed in this period, symbolising non-attachment and indifference towards the material world; (iii) the example of negative relation between the lotus and water emerges in this phase, wherein drops on the lotus leaf is the undying soul and the lotus is the body and lastly (iv) the lotus continues to serve as a simile, which is a continuation of the second phase.

Contrary to the Vedic literature in the Pāli Canons a development of thoughts regarding lotus does not exist as is found in the Vedic literature. The texts do not show any inclination towards myths or complicated symbolism of the lotus. Hence the references are simple and stereotyped. There is also absence of elaboration of the earlier conceptions and rituals as the Pāli canons do not deal with liturgy.

The most important role of the lotus in the Vedic literature is its symbolism in the cosmic evolution, whereas the Pāli Canons do not utter anything on problems regarding cosmogony, as the Buddha did not talk about these. The Lord advised his fellow monks not to speculate on the questions related to esoteric and metaphysics. He refused to speak on these subjects as these do not help in realising the ultimate goal - nirvāna.

A single thread of idea runs through most of the references regarding the lotus in the Vedic literature, which brings a kind of unity among the conceptions. But the references on lotus in the Pāli canons cannot be categorised like that as complicated symbolical role of this flower is not present. The Pāli canons had taken up only the latest ideas from the Vedic period. These are: (i) non-attachment and (ii) lotus as a standard of judgement for the appraisal of human beauty. Both the conceptions are continuations of the Vedic ideas. Similarly the role of the lotus (iii) in heightening one's beauty and (iv) as a decorative element has also their origin in the Vedas. Asvinā are called 'lotus-garlanded ones' (*puṣkara-srajau*) and the goddess Śrī-Lakṣmī enjoys the adjective *padma-mālinī* - the lady wearing a lotus garland. The association of lotus with Śrī-Lakṣmī and Asvinā has a deeper significance and its role as a beauty aid is of secondary importance. That holds true also in the case of lotus pond. The lotus-pond (*puṣkariṇī*) in the Vedas signifies a beautiful spot as well as immortality, whereas in the Pāli Canons the lotus garland as a beauty aid and lotus ponds as pleasure spots have no further significance. To these conceptions (v) birth inside a lotus due to meritorious deeds in the previous birth was introduced.

In one of the *Apadāna* stories, a Buddhist canonical text, various births of Therī Uppalavaṇṇā has been narrated (see supra p. 40). In one of her births she was born inside a lotus as she had offered fried corns covered with lotuses to a *paccekabuddha*. In a way it was a continuation of the Vedic idea of immortality, simplified and presented as a folk belief in the Pāli canons. A. Foucher[120] says, the conception of supernatural and divine birth on lotus goes back to Indian antiquity, i.e. before the Buddhist period. Buddhist art availed of this conception, which is reflected in the sculptures and plastic art of that period.

A contrast in the presentation of the idea of lotus-birth lies in the fact, that in the Vedic literature the lotus symbolises immortality and an actual flower is not meant as a receptacle. The case is otherwise in the Pāli canonical texts, where a flower in the nature is meant and it does not signify anything beyond it including immortality. The lotus-birth, mentioned in the Pāli Canons, had lost its philosophical substance of the Vedic period but the residue remained in the form of a folk-belief.

It is same in the case of lotus as a support. The Vedic seers did not mean the flower itself when they imagined a lotus as the seat or birthplace of the deities. Their sayings were reflections of their metaphysical conceptions, whereas in the *Jātaka* story a supernatural phenomenon was supposed to have occurred. The basic difference regarding the approach of the Vedic and Buddhist texts towards the lotus is due to the fact,

---

120 *The Beginning of Buddhist Art*, pp. 170 ṣ 173.

that the Vedic mantras are essentially metaphysical in character. On the other hand the *Jātakas* are popular tales[121], where supernatural happenings are told with a view to teach the folk about the fruits of good deeds. The Vedic priests regarded the lotus flower as something supernatural. Contrary to this, the monks regarded it as something very earthly and mundane. The Buddha and his fellow disciples chose examples from the common objects around them to drive the import of their sayings to the laity, who were not capable of understanding lofty philosophy or the intricacies of the various spiritual stages. Hence the lotus was chosen to help make a mental picture of the spiritual stages, as lotus was the most appreciated and common flower in those days, which is apparent from the innumerable references to it in the Pāli Canons.

This aquatic flower was appreciated, as we have discussed, by the Vedic priests as well as by the Buddha and his fellow monks and its different natural aspects inspired seers, priests, monks and the Lord to fasten various symbols and significance to this flower. Especially the priests had a very keen and subtle eye to observe those facts and drape them in mysterious language.

§ The lotus has its roots in the soil beneath the water but remains above it. The connection with earth below is not apparently visible and presents a picture of detachment. Because of its detached appearance lotus seems as if it is self-born on the surface of the water without roots and stalks. The mythical idea of self-creation has its root in this phenomenon. Prajāpati, the Creator, appeared first on a lotus (leaf) and is called *svayambhu* - the self-born and *kamalayonī* - the lotus-born. This is also the reason that the lotus was considered a suitable support for the terrestrial gods - Agni, Pṛthivī, Sarasvatī, Śrī-Lakṣmī or the Seer Vasiṣṭha. These gods particularly belong to this earth but they are also divine beings. They have their roots in this world but are beyond it. Bodhisattvas and seers like Vasiṣṭha can be placed in this category.

121 B.C. Law, *A History of Pali Literature*, Vol. 1, p. 272: "The *Jatakas* are highly important for the history of Buddhism, as they give an insight into popular Buddhism."

§ The lotus remains stable in the midst of unstable water. This inspired the seers and priests to imagine it as the support of the Earth, when it was floating helplessly on the primeval chaotic waters.

§ Defying its parentage - filthy and muddy water - the lotus looks like an embodied purity and hence it is called 'the essence of water'. The combination of soil and water generates fertility in the fields. For this reason lotus also symbolises fertility.

§ The different varieties of the family *Nymphaeaceae* open at different hours of the day and night. This fact was expressed in a mysterious language in the *Pañcaviṁśa Brāhmaṇa, Maitrāyaṇī Saṁhitā* and *Śatapatha Brāhmaṇa*. There it is said: 'They are the forms of heavenly bodies' and 'through the down shining of heavenly bodies the lotus springs up'.

§ The lotus is born of mud and water but it is completely free form these. The water glides off quickly from it. Similarly, desires roll off the mind of one who knows Brahman. This characteristic of the lotus also symbolises non-attachment of the Buddhist philosophy.

§ The lotus plant flourishes in water and is drenched with water. This aspect illustrates the spiritual stages in the Pali canons.

§ The scent belongs to the whole lotus flower and not to its any single part exemplifies the realisation by the person who meditates on the 'Five-Grasping-Groups'.

§ Lotus flower blossoms in a particular month in accordance to the laws of nature. This characteristic of the plant is cited to elucidate the adherence to the Rules of the Order by the followers of the Buddha, which they are not supposed to transgress.[122]

---

122 *yathāpi rammake māse bahu pupphanti vārija/*
natikkamanti taṁ māsaṁ samayo pupphanāya so//
tathā eva tvaṁ sākyaputta pupphita te vimuttiyā/
sāsanaṁ nātivattanti padumaṁ vārijaṁ yathā// *Thera Apadāna* 1.189-190.

5

Lotus in the Classical Sanskrit Literature

The classical Sanskrit literature abounds in references to various types of lotus, but its role is mostly limited to comparison, which has its root in the later period of the Vedic literature. In other words, the lotus serves as a standard of judgement for the assessment of human beauty. To the poets of this period lotus was an object of beauty and was treated accordingly. The different parts of a beautiful body, particularly face, eyes, hands and feet, were compared to the different parts and characteristics of the lotus, including its colour, petals and stalk.[123] With a rich store of synonyms at our disposal, it may be interesting to note how far the different names of lotus can be classified from the botanical point of view with the help of literary information. For this purpose it is necessary to know a few important and readily perceivable botanical data of the plant. Otherwise the exercise will be futile. Hence the main facts about this plant, which are of importance as far as literary evidences are concerned, are given in a nutshell.

As mentioned previously, by lotus an aquatic plant belonging to the family *Nymphaeaceae* is meant. Its two genera - *Nelumbo* (lotus) and *Nymphaea* (water lily) have five species in India. *Nelumbo* has only one species and *Nymphaea* has four. Flowers and leaves of *Nelumbo* open above the water, while those of *Nymphaea* float on the water surface:

---

123 Lotus is the blanket term used here for lotus and water lily both.

1. *Nelumbo nucifera*[124] - It is a large perennial water plant and is rooted in mud. The leaves of this species are 30-90 centimetres in diameter and have a soft velvety structure so that the leaves do not get wet on the upper surface. Its flowers are large, 10-25 centimetres in diameter, solitary, faintly odorous and are mostly red-rose or white in colour. There is a rare pale yellow variety also. The flowers and leaves open above the water.

2. *Nymphaea candida* [125]-. The flowers are white and have 12-20 petals. The petals are oblong to oblong-lanceolate and open during daytime.

3. *Nymphaea nouchali*[126] - This is a night-blooming variety of *Nymphaea*. Colours of the flowers of this species are either purplish-red or white and open at night. The flowers have 12-20 petals, which are narrowly oval and rounded at apex.

4. *Nymphaea stellata* - The flowers are usually blue, sometimes white or pink and open on three successive days from eight in the morning to two in the afternoon. The flowers have 10 to 16 lanceolate petals.

5. *Nymphaea tetragona*[127] - The flowers are comparatively small in size (3-8 centimetres) and open for 3-4 days from noon until five in the afternoon. These sweet-scented flowers are pure white in colour.

Before embarking on the classification of the Sanskrit names of lotus in the classical Sanskrit literature a discussion on the linguistic origin of these names, which might throw some light on the botanical data, may not be out of place. Not only modern linguists but the ancient scholars also gave some thoughts on the origin of these names. The famous lexicon of ancient India *Amarakoṣa* (6th Cen. A.D.) counts thirty-one names of lotus under *vārivarga* (water group). These are:

---

124 Also known as *Nelumbium speciosum.*

125 Also known as *Nymphaea alba*

126 Also known as *Nymphaea pubescens* or *Nymphea lotus*

127 Also known as *Nymphaea pygmea*

saugandhika, kahlāra, hallaka, raktasandhyaka, utpalȧ, kuvalaya, nīlāmbujanma, indīvara, kumuda, kairava, padma, nalina, aravinda, mahotpala, sahasrapatra, kamala, śatapatra, kuśeśaya, paṅkeruha, tāmarasa, sārasa, sarasīruha, bisaprasūna, rājīva, puṣkara, ambhoruha, puṇḍarīka, sitāmbhoja, raktasaroruha, raktotpala and *kokanada*[128].

Considered from the point of view of linguistic origin these names can be divided into two groups: (a) thirteen of these are of Indo-Aryan origin; (b) rest are of unknown, perhaps predominantly of non-Aryan origin. The names belonging to group (a) have been originally attributive adjectives, which became independent nouns by usage: (i) *saugandhika* – sweet-smelling; (ii) *raktasandhyaka* – resembling the evening glow; (iii) *nīlāmbujanma* – blue and water-born; (iv) *sahasrapatra* - thousand-petalled; (v) *śatapatra* – hundred-petalled; (vi) *kuśeśaya* – lying in water; (vii) *paṅkeruha* – growing in mud, (viii) *sārasa* – belonging to pond, (ix) *sarasīruha* – growing in pond, (x) *bisaprasūna* – flower of stalk, (xi) *ambhoruha* – growing in water, (xii) *sitāmbhoja* – white and water-born and (xiii) *raktasaroruha* – red and water-born.

The names *śatapatra, sahasrapatra, saugandhika* are descriptive and points to the number of petals, though exaggerated, or to its sweet scent. Others like *ambhoruha, paṅkeruha, sarasīruha, sārasa, bisprasūna* point to a characteristic of the family *Nyphaeacea,* i.e. the place where these plants grow. However, these expressions are not enough to point to genera of lotus or water lily. But in the case of *kuśeśaya* (lying in water) it can be said with some certainty that it indicates to a species of water lily, as the flowers and

---

128 *saugandhikaṁ tu kahlāraṁ hallakam raktasandhyakam/ syād utpalaṁ kuvalayam atha nīlāmbujanma ca // indīvaram ca nīle 'smin site kumudakairave/ vā puṁsi padmaṁ nalinam aravindam mahotpalam / sahasrapatraṁ kamalam śatapatraṁ kuśeśayam // paṅkeruhaṁ tāmarasaṁ sārasam sarasīruham/ bisaprasūna-rājīva-puṣkarāmbhoruhāṇi ca // puṇḍarīkaṁ sitambhojam atha raktasaroruhe / rakotpalaṁ kokanadam....//* Amarakoṣa 37 – 42.

leaves of *Nymphaea* float on the surface of water (see supra p.83). *Nilāmbujanma* (blue and water-born) is a name of *Nymphaea stellata*, as this alone has a blue variety. For *raktasandhyaka* (similar to evening glow) and *raktasaroruha* (red and water-born) first comes the purple variety in question. However *Nymphaea stellata* and *Nelumbo nucifera* both have a red variety. Again *sitāmbhoja* (white and water-born) utters too little as all the five species have flowers of this colour.

Bhānujī Dīkṣit's (17th century) commentary on *Amarakoṣa* gives Sanskrit derivations for four names of group (b). According to him: *halla vikasane (halla* means opening) is at the root of *hallaka; kairava* is derived from *ke jale rauti* (it roars in water); *kokanada* is from *kokān cakravākān nadati* (cries for *kokas* or *cakravākas*, kind of bird) and *padma* is derived from *pad* - to go. For *nalina, rājīva, indīvara* and *puṣkara* Sanskrit derivations are possible. *Nalina* can be connected with *naḍa* – reed, as Uhlenbeck, Mayrhofer and Lueders[129] suppose. Lueders is of the opinion that *l* in *nalina* originates from *ḷ*. Interchange of *ḍ* and *ḷ* is usual in the *Ṛg-Veda* and post-Ṛgvedic periods. *Rājīva* seems to have been derived from the Sanskrit word *rājī* – row, line opines Bhānujī Dīkṣit[130] as well as Peterson[131] and Uhlenbeck (from *ṛjyati* – to stretch, op cit). *Indīvara*, believes Peterson[132] consists of the word *indi-* with suffixes *va* and *ra*. But the meaning of the word *indi-* is unknown. Uhlenbeck, Wackernagel[133], Mayrhofer, and Bhānujī Dīkṣit are unanimous that the verb *puṣ* – to prosper, to nourish is at the root of the word *puṣkara*. Burrow[134] on the other hand surmises a Dravidian origin for *puṣkara* and

---

129 Uhlenbeck, Kurzgefasstes etymologisches Wörterbuch der altindischen Sprache; Mayrhofer, Etymologisches Wörterbuch des Altindischen; Lueders, Philologica Indica, p. 555.

130 *keśarasya rājy asyāsti*

131 IF, 34, p. 233

132 *Ibid*, 34, p. 233

133 Altindische Grammatik II/2, p.534

134 BSOAS, 12, 1947: *Dravidian Studies* VII, p.386.

connects it with the Tamil word *pokai* and Malayalam word *poyka* both mean pond, lake. According to him *y* in Tamil can represent a former sibilant.

The names presumably of Dravidian origin are: *kumuda, kuvalaya, kamala, tāmarasa* and *aravinda*. Burrow[135] connects *kumuda* with the Tamil word *kuvi* – to close as flowers by night, to assume a globular form. He thinks it indicates to the night lotus, which closes its petals at the daybreak. Wackernagel[136] is of the opinion that *kumuda* is derived from the word *mud* – to be happy. Monier-Williams in his Sanskrit-English Dictionary, gives the meaning of *kumuda* as 'exciting, what joy'. To Burrow *kuvalaya* is a variation of the Tamil name for blue lotus *kuvalai* and *kamala* is a phonetic variation of the same Tamil word. In Kannada blue water lily is called *komale*. In the Sanskrit-English Dictonary by Monier-Williams *kamala* also means 'pale-red, rose-coloured'. Mayrhofer and Burrow[137] think *tāmarasa* is connected with the Tamil word *tāmarai* – lotus. Śabara in his *Śabarabhāsya*, a commentary on the *Mīmāṁsāsūtra* mentions that *tāmarasa* is a non-Aryan (*mleccha*) word. Burrow[138] thinks *aravinda* is derived from the Telgu word *araviri* – a half-opened flower. Lotus is so called as it remains open only for half day and the suffix *–vinda* is a contracted participial of Tamil word *virinta*.

Multiple explanations are available for *puṇḍarika, utpala* and *kahlāra*. Grassamnn[139] derives *puṇḍarika* from the Sanskrit word *puṇḍa* – mark, sign. Burrow[140] connects this word with the Dravidian word *puṇḍari* – water, lake, pond, whereas Weber[141] and Wackernagel[142] connect it with *pāṇḍu* – white, yellowish. S.K. Chatterjee[143] thinks *utpala* has its origin in the

---

135 *Ibid*, 11, 1943, DS III, p. 135, Transaction of Philological Society, 1946, p.9
136 *Op cit*. P. 70.
137 Transaction of Philological Society, 1946, p. 9
138 BSOAS, 12, p. 366
139 Wörterbuch zum Rigveda
140 BSOAS, 12 p.385
141 Indische Studien, IV, p. 417
142 Altindische Grammatik, I, p. 170
143 Calcutta Review, Sept. 1923, p. 453

Munda word *upal-ba*, which means a floating flower. Mayrhofer and Uhlenbeck connect it with the Sanskrit word *utpata* – flying upwards, i.e. opening as also Monier-Williams and Uhlenbeck think. Turner[144] is of the view that *kahlāra* cannot be an Aryan word because of *ṛ* in its Maithili form *kaṛhāra*. Wackernagel[145] supposes a Kashmiri origin due to – *hl-* in *kahlāra*.

The different names discussed above hardly furnish any clue with the help of which a Sanskrit name of lotus can be connected with one of the species of the family *Nymphaeacea* found in India, barring of course a few like *kuśeśaya* or *nīlāmbujanma*. Hence with the help of illustrative statements from the classical Sanskrit literature an attempt has been made to classify the familiar names of lotus from the botanical point of view[146].

But before proceeding to classify the names based on the data furnished in the texts of the classical period, selected randomly, it is worthwhile to refresh our observations about the few synonyms of this flower we have already come across in the Vedic literature and Pāli Canons. It has been observed that *puṣkara* is the original denomination used for the lotus flower in the *Ṛg-veda*. This very important denomination retains its prime position throughout the Vedic literature. In the post-Ṛgvedic period another important name - *puṇḍarīka* - crops up. It is also mentioned in the *Ṛg-Veda* but only in a supplementary hymn *Śrī-Sūkta*, which belongs to a much later period. *Puṇḍarīka* comes in the *Atharva-Veda,* in the books of *Yajur-Veda* (*Taittirīya Saṁhitā, Vājasneyī Saṁhitā* and *Maitrāyaṇī Saṁhitā*), *Brāhmaṇas, Āraṇyakas* and *Upaniṣads.*

---

144 A Comparative Dictionary of Indo-Aryan Languages.

145 Altindische Grammatik, I, p. 244.

146 Richard Schmidt (Beiträge zur Flora Sanskritika, III, "Der Lotus in der Sanskrit Literatur" in ZDMG 67, 1913, pp.462-470) and Wilhelm Rau (Asiatika – Festschrift Friedrich Weller, pp. 505-513) have handled this problem of classification of Sanskrit names. Schmidt gives corresponding botanical names to the Sanskrit names of the lotus and water lily as far as these are mentioned in Roth and Böthlingk's Sanskrit Wörterbuch. Rau classifies according to different colours of the genera *Nymphaea* and *Nelumbo.*

In the Vedic literature lotus has not been presented as a mere flower but as the support of divinities or cosmos, which has been discussed in the foregoing pages. Whenever it has been thought as a support the name *puṣkara* has been used in the Vedic literature. *Puṇḍarīka* has been used as a class name and there it denotes the family *Nymphaeaceae*, which includes lotus (*Nelumbo*) as well as water lily (*Nymphaea*). In support of this view lines from the *Maitrāyaṇī Saṁhitā* (4.4.7) and *Pañchaviṁśa Brāhmaṇa* (18.9.6) may be quoted: 'through the down-shining of the heavenly bodies *pundarika* is born', or '*puṇḍarīkāṇi* (pl. of *puṇḍarīka*) are an appearance of heaven, an appearance of heavenly bodies', says the *Śatapatha Brāhmaṇa* (5.4.5.14). Heavenly bodies include the sun, moon and stars. Hence *puṇḍarīka* stands for lotus and water lily in general in the Vedic literature, as the latter one has a variety, which opens at night (*Nymphaea nouchali*).

The description of the lotus as a flower is not found in the Vedic literature because of the symbolic value attached to it. There hardly anything is uttered directly on their botanical characteristics with exception only in a few passages that too in the later stage of the Vedic literature. *Chāndogya Upaniṣad* mentions red colour of *puṇḍarīka* (*kapyāsam puṇḍarīkam* – 1.6.7) and *Atharva-Veda* mentions the sweet scent of *puṣkara* (see p.18).

Other names found in the Vedic literature are *kumuda, padma, saroja* and *sarasīja*. *Kumuda* is mentioned in the *Atharva-Veda* along with its roots, stalks and fibres (4.34.5). *Padma* surfaces in the *Śrī-Sūkta*, where limbs and the skin colour of Śrī have been compared to *padma*. It can be inferred that by *padmavarṇā* (see p.55) the poet means the rose colour of the skin. Hence *padma* points to the red-rose colour of *Nelumbium speciosum*. *Padma* in conjunction with *āsana* (sitting posture) has been mentioned in a hymn in the *Maitrāyaṇī Saṁhitā* (2.9.1), in which four-faced Brahma is said to have a lotus-seat (*padmāsana*). *Saroja* and *sarasīja*, mentioned in the *Śrī-Sūkta*, means water-born, which are synonyms of the lotus. In the Buddhist literature a group of words - *uppala paduma puṇḍarīka* (Skt. *utpala padma puṇḍarīka*) - occur very often and means blue, red and white variety of lotus. Or it can be said that *uppala paduma puṇḍarīka* is a blanket term used for different kinds of lotus.

With different names of lotus new words were coined, such as *padminī, nalinī, kumudinī, utpalinī, puṣkariṇī*. These words mean host of *padma, nalina, kumuda, utpala* or *puṣkara* (varieties of lotus) respectively or ponds teeming with one of these varieties. In the *Ṛg-Veda* and *Atharva-Veda puṣkariṇī* denotes a pond abounding in lotus. But *pokkhariṇī*, the Pāli form of *puṣkariṇī*, means pond in general with or without lotuses, whereas Pāli *uppalinīyam, padumінīyam, puṇḍarikinīyam* signify ponds having specific varieties of lotus - blue, red and white respectively.

Many synonyms of the lotus, which are mentioned in the books of classical Sanskrit literature, were originally attributive adjectives, which became independent by usage. Among these most common are *paṅkaja, paṅkeruha* (mud-born), *abja, ambhoja, ambhoruha* (water-born), *kuśeśaya* (lying on water), *nilāmbujanma* (blue and water-born) and many such other names. Now in our attempt to classify the names we want to turn to the poets of the classical period. But it must be remembered that the poets in accordance to their poetic intentions were far from furnishing exact data; they rather tended to exaggerate. Nevertheless, occasionally they did mention an interesting botanical fact in support of their sayings, which we will see presently.

† ***abja, ambhoja*** : Poet Kālidāsa calls the rising sun the 'friend of *abjas*' (*Raghuvaṁśam* 4.61 - *bālātapam ivābjānām akālajaladodayaḥ* – as the young sun, the friend of *abjas*, does not bear the rising of out of season clouds). Māgha, another poet, says *ambhoja* opens its petals with the rising sun (*Śiśupālavadham* 11.64 - *śrīmad ambhojaṣaṇḍam*). The two poets allude to the same time for the opening of the petals. *Abja* and *ambhoja* may be Sanskrit names of *Nymphaea stellata*, which opens from eight in the morning till two in the afternoon.

† ***aravinda*** : 'Pārvati's body was brought to development by adolescence as the *aravinda*s by the rays of the sun' observes Kālidāsa in his poetic composition *Kumārasambhavam* (*sūryāṁśubhir bhinnam ivāravindam*-1.32). Except *Nymphaea nouchali* all the other species blossom during daytime. In the absence of a more definite clue *aravinda* may be a name of any of the four varieties.

† ***indīvara*** : Undoubtedly it is a name of blue *Nymphaea stellata*, since Kālidāsa describes the skin-colour of the king as *indīvara-śyāma-tanuḥ* (*Raghuvaṁśam* 6.65 - the king, whose body is like blue *indīvara*). Another fact that this variety opens its petals during daytime is also alluded to in a couplet in *Śṛṅgāratilakam* (155): '*indīvara*s, which have the same beauty as your eyes, are drowned in water'[147], says the poet, as the *nāyikā* had closed her eyes because it was night.

† ***utpala*** : 'The traveller weeps, seeing the beauty of black (read blue) eyes of his beloved in the *utpala*s' (*asita-nayana-lakṣmīm lakṣyatvotpaleṣu* - 3.24), observes Kālidāsa in his poetic composition *Ṛtusaṁhāram*. Though *utpala* generally points to the blue variety of *Nymphaea stellata*, still often poets prefix *nīla* or *asita* (blue) to emphasise the colour. Thus there are synonyms like *nīlotpala* and *asitotpala*. *Rakta, aruaṇa, lohita* (red) or *śveta* (white) are also prefixes of *utpala*. *Raktotpala, asitotpala, lohitotpala* may indicate *Nymphaea nouchali*, as the flowers of this species are either purplish-red or white.

Māgha alludes to a botanically interesting characteristic of *mahotpala*: "the *mahotpala* sank in the moving water" in *Śiśupālavadham* (*ālole payasi mahotpalam mamajja*- 3.48). Conrad[148] says that the petals of *Nelumbo* fall down when full blown. *Mahotpala* is said to open its petals by the rays of the sun: "open your eyes as the lotus plant opens the petals of *mahotpala* in the morning" (*mahotpalam pratyuṣasīva padminī*

---

147 *yat tvan netra-samāna-kānti salile magnam tad indīvaram /*
megheir antaritiḥ priye tava mukhachāyānukāri śaśī // Śṛgāratilakam 155
148 The Waterlilies, p.4.

– *Vikramorvaśīyam* 1.5). This denomination, can be said, is one of the Sanskrit names of *Nelumbo nucifera*, a day lotus. Māgha gives a poetic tinge to the natural fact.

† ***kamala*** : The redness of *kamala* (*raktatvam kamalānām* - *Nītiśatakam* 17) is an accepted fact and it blossoms during daytime, as Kālidāsa indicates this indirectly in the *Meghadūtam*. He says, '*kamala* does not display its beauty after the departure of the sun' (*sūryapāye na khalu kamalam puṣ yati svām abhikhyām* -2.20). Sometimes it is qualified with the word *rakta* (red) and hence *kamala* and *raktakamala* may indicate the red variety of *Nymphaea stellata* or *Nelumbo nucifera*. The yellow variety of *Nelumbo nucifera* has the Sanskrit names like *kanakakamala, hemāmbuja, hemapadma* as no other Indian species has a yellow variety.

† ***kumuda*** : Kālidāsa says, 'only moonbeams can open the petals of *kumuda* and not the rays of the sun' (*nocchvasiti tapanakiranaiś candrasyaivāṁśubhiḥ kumudam* - *Vikramorvaśīyam* 3.16). In the *Meghadūtam* the same poet compares white glances of *śaphara* fish with the whiteness of *kumuda (kumudaviśadāni* – 1.43*)*. It seems *kumuda* is a Sanskrit name of white *Nymphaea nouchali,* which opens its petals at night touched by moonbeams. (In Sanskrit *kaumudī* means moonbeams, which is derived from *kumuda*, as it causes this variety to blossom.)

† ***kuvalaya*** : Dark clouds have been compared to the petals of *kuvalaya* in *Ṛtusaṁhāram* (*kuvalaya-dala-nīlaiḥ* – 2.22). Hence it is another synonym of blue *Nymphaea stellata*, the only species having a blue variety.

† ***kuśeśaya*** : *kuśeśaya-tāmra-talena* (*Raghuvaṁśam* 6.18) observes Kālidāsa, which means that the palms were red like *kuśeśaya*. It may be either *Nymphaea nouchali* or *Nymphaea stellata*, since both have a red variety. It cannot be a synonym for *Nelumbo nucifera* as the word *kuśeśaya* means 'lying in water', whereas *N. nucifera* opens above the water.

† ***kairava*** : Bhartṛhari in his *Nītiśatakam* says, 'the moon succeeds in opening the petals of *kairava* (*candro vikāsayati kairavacakravālam* - 74). *Amarakoṣa*, an old Sanskrit lexicon,

mentions white as the colour of *kumuda* and *kairava* (*site kumuda-kairave*). Hence *kairava* like *kumuda* is another name of white *Nymphea nouchali*.

† ***kokanada*** : Kṛṣṇa very artfully mentions the change of the colour of the eyes of Rādhā due to anger, observes Jaideva in his poetic creation *Gītagovindam*. Kṛṣṇa says, 'though her eyes possess a shade of blue, they are taking the colour of a *kokanada* (*nīlanalinābham api tanvi tava locanam dhārayati kokanadarūpam* - 10.5). Both *Nymphaea stellata* and *Nelumbo nucifera* have a red variety. Hence it can be a synonym of either of the two.

† ***paṅkaja*** : The sleeping beauty of a *nāyika's* face is compared to *paṅkaja*, which closes its petals at night: *niśi suptam ivaika pankajam* (*Raghuvaṁśam* 8.55). Four species of the family *Nymphaeaceae* blossom during daytime. It seems *paṅkaja* is a blanket term denoting lotus or waterlily.

† ***padma*** : A very interesting botanical fact has been mentioned by the poet Aśvaghoṣa in his literary work *Saundarānandam* (13.5): ' As a lotus leaf, though born in water and remain in water, is not stained by water either above or below' (*padmaparṇam yathā caiva jale jātam jale sthitam/ upariṣṭād adhastād va na jalenopalipyate*). *Majjhima Nikāya*, a Pāli text also says, the leaves of *padma* stand a little above the surface of water (*isakopaṇe paduminipatte* - Sūtra 152). These two characteristics, specially the second one, tally with that of a *Nelumbo nucifera*. *Padma* is of red colour, says Kālidasa in his play *Abhijñāna-Śākuntalam*, where the king Duṣyanta expresses the redness ofs Śakuntalā's feet as *padma-tāmrau* (3.20). With almost certainty, it can be said that *padma* stands for the red variety of *Nelumbo nucifera*.

In the books of Pāli Canons *paduma* often stands for the lotus in general and its variety is suggested by another denomination of lotus such as *śatapatra-padumam, kokanada-padumam, uppala-padumam* etc (Tha. Ap 34.2; 392.6; SN 3.2.2.12). Besides *paduma* is sometimes qualified with words *pañcavidha, pañcavaṇṇa* or *nānā*, which shows that by *paduma* often the family *Nymphaeacea* is meant.

† ***puṇḍarīka*** **:** Poet and playwright Māgha writes: 'As if at the daybreak the impassioned sun having squeezed the moon cruelly by his hands, scatters the essence of beauty, which is white like the fresh water from the clouds, inside *puṇḍarīka'* [149] (*Śiśupālavadham* - 11.62). In non-poetic simple language it means *puṇḍarīka* is white (like the moon) and opens its petals when the sun rises. Only these two data are not sufficient to determine the species, as four of the five species of the family *Nymphaeaceae* have white varieties and open during daytime (except the night water lily *Nymphaea nouchali*). In the Vedic literature also *puṇḍarīka* does not point to a particular variety of lotus but is used as a blanket term for all the varieries including *Nymphaea nouchali*, which opens its petals at night. There it is said: "Lotuses are appearances of heaven, appearances of heavenly bodies". [150] Heavenly bodies include the sun, moon and the stars.

† ***puṣkara*** **:** *Chāndogya Upaniṣad* mentions a botanical fact about *puṣkara*. It says: As water does not cling to the leaf of a *puṣkara* (*yathā puṣkara-palāsa āpo na śliṣyante* - 4.14.3). It may be a name of *Nelumbo nucifera,* which has the same characteristic.

† ***sarasīja*** **:** 'The petals of *sarasīja* open by the rays of the sun', says Kālidasa in his epic poem *Raghuvaṁśam* (*sarasījair aruṇaṁśubhinnaiḥ* -5.69). Like *puṇḍarīka* it may indicate any variety of lotus or water lily.

We have seen that the poets of the classical period sometimes described the flowers faithfully with regard to natural facts and thereby striking upon some botanically valuable data, with the help of which a few Sanskrit names could be identified with one or the other species of the family *Nymphaeacea*.

---

149 *adayam iva karāgrair niṣpīḍya sadyaḥ śaśadharam aharādam rāgavān uṣ ṇaraśmih /*
avakirati nitāntam kānti-niryāsam abda-sruta-navajala-pāṇḍum puṇḍarīkodareṣu // Śiśupālavadham 11.62

150 See supra p. 41ff.

Bibliography

Original Texts

Abhijñānaśākuntalam, Ed. by C. R. Devadhar, New Delhi

Agnipurāṇa, Anadasrama Sanskrit Series 41, Poona 1900

Amarakoṣa, Ed. by A.A. Ramnathan, Madras

Aṅguttaranikāya, Ed. by R. Morris and E. Hardy, Pali Text Society (PTS), London 1883-1910

Atharvaveda-Saṁhitā, Ed. by Pt. Shankara, N.S. Press, Bombay 1895-98

Bhagavadgīta, Gita Press, Gorakhpur, 1953

Chāndogya Upaniṣad, Ed. by S. Radhakrishnan, London 1953

Dīghanikāya, Ed. by T.N. Rhys-Davis and J.E. Carpenter, PTS, London 1903-32

Gītagovindam, Ed. by C. Lassen, Bonn

Jātaka, Ed. by V. Fausboll, London 1877-97

Kaivalya Upaniṣad, Ed. by S. Radhakrishnan, London 1953

Kumārasambhavam, Ed. by K.P. Parab, Bombay 1893

Lalitavistara, Ed. by S. Lefmann, Halle 1902

Mahābhārata, Ed. by T.R. Krishnacharya and T.R. Vyasacharya, Bombay 1908

Mahāniddesa, Ed. by L. de la Vallee Poussin and E.J. Thomas, PTS,London 1916

Maitrāyaṇi-Saṁhitā, Ed. by L. von Schroeder, Leipzig 1891-35

Maitrāyaṇi-Upaniṣad, Ed. by S. Radhakrishnan, London 1953

Majjhimanikāya, Ed. by V. Trenkner and R. Chalmers, PTS, London 1885-1925

Meghadutam, Ed. by M.R. Kale, Bombay

Nirukta, Anandashrama Sanskrit Series 83, Poona 1921-22

Nītiśatakam, Ed. by Krishna Shastri, Bombay 1888

Pañcaviṁśa-Brāhmaṇa, Ed by Anandachandra Vedantavagisha, Calcutta 1870-71

Petavatthu, Ed. by Minayeff, PTS, London 1888

Raghuvaṁśam, Ed. by K.P. Parab, Bombay 1891

Rāmāyaṇa, Gita Press, Gorakhpur

Ṛgveda-Saṁhitā, Ed. by F. Maxmueller, London 1890-92

Ṛtusaṁhāram & Sṛṇgāratilakm, Ed. by S. Panasikara, Bombay 1922

Saṁyuttanikāya, Ed. by L. Freer, PTS, London 1884-98

Śatapatha-Brāhmaṇa, Ed. by Albrecht Weber, Berlin 1855

Saundarananda, Ed. by E.H. Jhonston, London 1928

Śiśupālavadham, Ed. by Durgaprasad and Shivdatta, Bombay 1888

Taittirīya Āraṇyaka, Ed. by R.L. Mitra, Calcutta 1872

Taittirīya Brāhmaṇa, Ed. by R.L. Mitra, Calcutta 1859-62

Taittirīya Saṁhitā, Ed. by E. Roer, E.B. Cowell and M. Nyayaratna, Calcutte 1860-99

Thera Apadāna, Theri Apadana, Ed. by Mary E. Lilley, PTS, London 1925-27

Vājasneyī Saṁhitā, Ed. by Ram Sakala Misra, Benaras 1912-15

Vikramorvaśīyam, Ed. by S.P. Pandit, Bombay 1879

Vimānavatthu, Ed by R.R. Gunaratne, PTS, London 1886

Vinayapiṭaka (5 Vols.) Ed. by H. Oldenberg, PTS, London 1879-83

Secondary Literature

Biswas, K. & C. Calder, *Handbook of common water and marsh plants of India and Burma*, Calcuttta 1955

Bosch, F.D.K., *The Golden Germ* 's-Gravenhage 1960

Burrow, *Dravadian Studies* in **Bulletin of the School of Oriental and African Studies, (BSOAS)**

Chalmers, R., *Further Dialogues of the Buddha* (2 Vols.), Trans. of *Majjhimanikaya* SBB, 1926-27

Conrad, H.S., *The Waterlilies*, Washington 1905

Coomaraswamy, A.K., *Elements of Buddhist Iconography*, Cambridge (Mass.) 1935

Coomaraswamy, A.K., *Origin of the Buddha Image*, University of Calcutta 1970

Coomaraswamy, A.K., *Origin of lotus-(so-called Bell) capitals* by in **Indian Historical Quarterly (IHQ)**, Vol. VI

Craven, R.C., *Indian Art*, Lonon 1976

Cultural Heritage of India, Vol.I, II, Ramakrishna Mission Institute of Culture, Calcutta

Dasgupta, S.N., *A History of Indian Philosophy*, Cambridge 1951

Eggeling, J., *Shatapatha Brahmana,* (Trans.), SBE

Eugler, A. & E. Gilg, *Syllabus der Pflanzenfamilie,* Berlin 1924

Fergusson, James, *Indian and Eastern Art*, Vol. 1

Foucher, A. & J. Marshall *The Monuments of Sanchi*, Vol. II

Foucher, A., *The Beginning of Buddhist Art*

Geldner, K.F., *Der Rigveda* (translation of the Rigveda), Goettingen 1923

Goetz, H., *Indien*, Baden-Baden, Germany

Gonda, J., *Aspects of Early Vishnuism*, Utrecht 1954

Grassmann, H., *Das Wörterbuch zum Rigveda*, Wiesbaden 1955

Griffith, R.T.H., *The Hymns of Atharvaveda* (2 Vols.), (Trans. of AV), Banaras 1916

Hartmann, Gerda, *Beiträge zur Gecshichte der Göttin Laksmi* Kiel 1933

Havell, E.B., *A Handbook of Indian Art*, Varanasi 1972

Hooker, J.D., *Flora of British India,* Vol. I, London 1957

Hopkins, E.W., *Epic Mythology,* Strassburg 1915

Ions, Veronica, *Indische Mythologie*, Wiesbaden 1967

Jataka, Trans. by Chalmers, Cowell, Francis, Neil & Rouse, SBB, 1895-1907

Keith, A.B., *Veda of Black Yajus School*, Harvard 1914

Law, B.C., *A History of Pali Literature* London 1933

Lueders, H., *Philologica Indica*, Göttingen

Macdonell, A.A., *A Vedic Reader*, Madras 1957

Macdonell, A.A., *Vedic Mythology,* Strassburg 1897

Marshall, J., *Cambridge History of India*

Mayrhofer, M., *Etymologisches Wörterbuch* , Heidelberg 1956

Mitra, A.K. *A Bell-Capital from Bhuvaneshwar* in **Indian Historical Quarterly (IHQ)**, Vol. V

Monier-Williams, *Sanskrit - English Dictionary*

Morenz, S. & J. Scubert, *Der Got auf derBlume*, Ascona, Switzerland

Mrs Rhys Davis, *Psalms of Brethern,* Trans. of *Theragāthā*, PTS, 1913

Mrs Rhys Davis, *Psalms of Sisters,* Trans. of *Therīgāthā*, PTS, 1909

New Larousse Encyclopaedia of Mythology, Feltham, England 1983

Oldenberg, H., *Die vedische Worte fuer 'schön' und 'Schönheit'* in **Nachrichten der Göttinger Gesellschaft der Wissenschaft (NGGW)**, Berlin, 1918

Petersson **(IF)**, **Indogermanische Forschung**, 34

Radhakrishnan, S., *Indian Philosophy* (2 Vols.), George Allen & Unwin, London

Radhakrishnan, S., *The Principal Upanisads*, London 1953

Rao, T.A.G., *Elements of Hindu Iconography*, Varanasi Delhi 1971

Rhys Davis and Oldenberg, *The Vinaya Texts* (3 Vols.), Trans. of *Vinayapiṭaka*, SBE, 1881-85

Rhys Davis, T.W., *Dialogues of the Buddha*, Trans. of *Dīghanikāya*, London 1951

Scheftelowitz, *Śrī-Sūkta* in **Zetschrift der deutschen morgenländischen Gesellschaft** (ZDMG) 75, Leipzig

Scheftelowitz, J., *Die Apokryphen des Ṛgveda*, Breslau 1906

Schumann, H.W., *Der Historische Buddha*, Munich 1995

Uhlenbeck, C.C., *Kurzgefasstes etymologisches Wörterbuch der altindischen Sprache*, Amsterdam 1898-99

Wackernagel, *Altindische Grammatik*, Göttingen 1896-1905

Weber, *Indische Studien*

Winternitz, M, *A History of Indian Literature* (2 Vols.), Calcutta 1933, 1959

Woodward and Rhys Davids, *The Book of Kindred Sayings* (5 Vols), Trans. of *Samyuttanikāya*, 1917-30

Woodward and Rhys Davis, *The Book of Gradual Sayings* (5 Vols), Trans. of *Aṅguttaranikāya*, PTS 1932-36

Zimmer, H., *Mythen und Symbole in indischer Kunst und Literatur*, Zurich MCMLI

Index